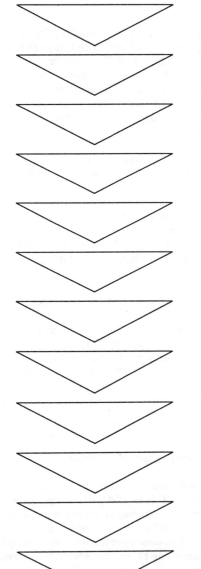

Second Edition
Understanding & Reducing Your Home Electric Bill

Richard L. Hepburn, B.S., M.S.

Edited by Christopher Carson and Patrick Zale

Graphics by J.K. Barefield

Copyright © 1996 Emerald Ink Publishing
Houston, Texas

For more information, call 1-800-324-5663 or write:
Emerald Ink Publishing, 7141 Office City Drive, Suite 220
Houston, Texas 77087.

Library of Congress Cataloging-in-Publication Data
Hepburn, Richard L. (Richard Leroy), 1932 -
    Understanding & reducing your home electric bill / Richard
  L. Hepburn; edited by Christopher Carson and Patrick Zale;
  graphics by J.K. Barefield.
      p. cm.
  Includes bibliographical references (p. 140) and Index.
  ISBN 1-885373-01-5
  1. Dwellings -- Energy conservation. 2. Electric Power
-- Conservation. 3. Electric power consumption --
United States -- Costs. I. Carson, Christopher, 1949   - .
II. Zale, Patrick, 1957 -   . III. Title. IV. Title: Understanding
and reducing your home electric bill.
TJ163.5.D86H457   1996
6969—dc20   06-25263 CIP

Printed and bound in the United States of America.

This book is designed to provide accurate and authoritative information on the subject matter covered. It is sold with the understanding that the publisher is not engaged in rendering legal or other professional services. If legal advice or other expert assistance is required, the services of a competent professional person should be sought. While every attempt has been made to provide accurate information, the author or publisher cannot be held accountable for errors or omissions.

About This Book

Author Hepburn, a utility consultant to major industry in Texas, wrote this book to distill the decade's developments in home energy products and strategies.

Read this book to reduce the amount of electricity you use in your home while maintaining or improving the quality of life, then use the money you save on something else. This book can help you understand how technology and inventiveness have made it possible to save money on electric bill expenditures without affecting comfort or safety.

Now you can determine if you can—or want—to save money on electric bills without cutting back on necessary usage. This book:

- Although written specifically for homeowners, also applies to businesses.
- Clarifies the nature of electrical usage and consumption in the home, discusses cost-saving strategies and energy saving devices currently available.
- Contains phone numbers and addresses of companies making or selling products of interest
- Allows you to find the right "mix" of interest and involvement for you.

If you own a home or small business, you can probably reduce your electric bill significantly with the information in this book. But you *will* positively understand how you can pare down your electric bill at home and use that money for something else!

About the Author

A word or two of explanation and background about the author should give the reader some idea about Richard L. Hepburn. First, he is a third generation native Californian. After five years at UCLA (two years in pursuit of geology and then three more years and three summer sessions), he earned a BS in Engineering. He worked for seven months for the L.A. Dept. of Water & Power building steam-powered electric power plants. He then entered the US Air Force pilot training program. When he received his wings he chose jet fighter training, F-86 then F-100 (which held the world speed record at that time). After 10 years in the USAF, he got tired of *just* flying, especially since the USAF sent him back to school for an MS in Engineering. So he got out of the USAF to pursue an engineering career.

He worked for several major aerospace companies. After about five years at each company, he wanted some new challenges. As a result, he worked in several areas of engineering, the mix resulting in a broad, if not too deep, exposure to *many* fields of manufacturing, science and engineering. He is a "broad brush" man, without profound depth in any one area but with some acquaintance with a large variety of fields of endeavor.

Thus, when Utility Consultants of Houston asked him to do an energy reduction study for a large Holiday Inn, and then for a manufacturer of vertical venetian blinds, he was able to prepare studies for each. Although the studies were not extremely detailed, they both offered suggestions which could substantially reduce the electric bills of the clients substantially. The study for the manufacturer inspired Emerald Ink Publishing to ask him to expand it into a book for commercial customers of the local electric utility company. The book is now carried at a few Houston technical book stores and via the internet. Having tasted of writing as a career, he immersed himself in the challenge to write something useful to nearly everyone. He kept it simple and yet explained complicated concepts. Explicit suggestions should permit most readers to save the cost of the book nearly every month of the year! That is indeed the goal.

Acknowledgements

To my wonderful wife Gloria and all my family who put up with me while writing and researching the subject, I dedicate this book.

I am deeply indebted to Chris Carson of Emerald Ink Publishing for his prodding, encouragement and editorial help. Of course, we wouldn't have a book without J.K. Barefield who put it all together in printable form.

To Gayle West with DuroTest for his enthusiastic and expert assistance on lighting.

To Yung S. Choi at Heat Pipe Technology, Harry Featherston at ThermoRider, Inc. and Keith Quinten at Utility Consultants of Houston, and all the others too numerous to mention but irreplaceable for their input and support.

Table of Contents

Introduction

Why Try?

Some may ask, "Why even try?" Many of us may think that our electric bill is, somehow, immutable and unchangeable. Well, yes, we could turn off all of the lights, or kick all of the teenagers out of our home just to save electricity. But, of course, nothing like that is really practical.

However, most of us are actually able to pay our electric bill each month without undue hardship. We do, naturally, complain that it is too "high" and that it seems to keep going up and up. It would be "nice" to have a lower electric bill, especially if it is not too hard to achieve or too expensive!

This book will give you some motivation beyond just the dollars to be saved. First, some economic "facts of life": the people who build houses, apartments and mobile homes are in business—which means that they are trying to make money. The way businesses do this is by making a product that people are more willing to buy than a similar product from the competition. In addition, they must see to it that their cost is less than their selling price. Thus, the motivation to provide the most desirable house, from the public's standpoint, at the lowest possible cost. Since the public does not yet demand highly energy efficient housing, the builders do not provide it! Thus, many architects and builders have not yet been forced by economics to know "all about" high efficiency technology.

Since the public does not yet demand highly energy efficient housing, the builders do not provide it.

Some Real Life Numbers

Let's look at some numbers. One 100 watt light bulb consumes or uses one kwh (*kilowatt-hour*) of electrical energy when it burns for ten hours. This translates to 876 kwh in a year of continuous illumination (24 hrs x 365 days). "So what?" you may say. Well, that 876 kwh required 876 pounds of coal be consumed during the generation of electrical energy! Now if 2000 people left a 100 watt light on for a whole year that would consume 876 tons of coal in a year, and, if 2,283,105 people left a 100 watt light on for a year, it would consume one million tons of coal.

You can also conclude that if 2 million people SAVE 100 watts each hour of each day it saves a million tons of coal.

How much is "a million tons of coal"?

The USA burned 817 million tons of coal in 1994.

To give you some idea of whether "one million tons of coal" is "a lot" or not, the entire USA burned 817 million tons of coal in 1994. This amount of coal generated about 94% of all the electricity used in the USA in 1994. So, a million ton is about 1/1000th of our annual coal consumption in the US. It is fairly significant!

What does all this mean?

Even if you didn't follow all those figures above you can see that even a little bit of conservation by each of us adds up to a lot! Not only that but, at an average of eight to twelve cents for each kwh we use, saving 876 kwh represents a reduced cost to us of $70 to $100. Now that's not enough to send the kids to college, but in ten years it might add up to around $1000. If you can achieve such savings without having to work too hard or invest too much, it might just be worth it.

What about the Environment?

We have not yet discussed the environment. Although it is still somewhat controversial, it sure appears to me that the earth is warming up. This is referred to as Global Warming. The temperature has increased 4 degrees Fahrenheit since the ice age (18 million years ago). That change pales in comparison to the predictions of many today.

Power plants generate about a pound of carbon dioxide for each pound of fossil fuel[1] burned. CO_2, along with the other combustion products, is believed to trap the heat which previously radiated from the earth through the atmosphere into "empty space." This former heat loss presumably maintained the temperature of the earth at equilibrium. This accumulation of CO_2 results in what is described as the *greenhouse effect*. (A greenhouse stays warm by letting in the sun's heat and "keeping" much of it.)

So if, in our efforts to conserve and save money, we save a ton of coal, we also save more than a ton of CO_2 from being "dumped" into the atmosphere. This will in turn reduce—or at least not increase—the greenhouse effect.

Another "New" concept for us!

Any of us who have been involved in some sort of business have probably come across the concept of Life Cycle Cost. I certainly have. But as recently as six or seven years ago I had need of a window air conditioner. My only concern at that time was my instant, out-of-pocket expense. So I found a five or six year old a/c that seemed to be in good shape and bought it for a modest cost. I used it for about three seasons before it quit. The life cycle cost of that unit consisted of the low purchase price plus the very high cost of operation divided by its very short life. The cost per year was quite high but I did not con-

> The life cycle cost consisted of the low purchase price plus the high cost of operation divided by its very short life.

---

1. Fossil fuel is coal, oil or gas. These are believed to be the fossilized remains of prehistoric plants and/or animals.

sider that at the time of purchase, only the low out-of-pocket cost. It was a bad economic decision and one that was not beneficial to the environment.

Life Cycle Cost is a truly FUNDAMENTAL concept that is frequently involved in reducing your overall cost of electric energy.

I hope that the financial motivation, along with the benefit to the environment, will give most of us several reasons to consider putting the suggestions in this book into practice.

What's next?

To look forward, we will talk about your electric bill and what you can learn from it. Then we will look at air conditioning and heating. Next we will discuss lighting and how you can reduce that part of your bill. After that we will list several interesting and energy reducing "gadgets." Anything that seems to me to be too laborious[1] or too detailed will be relegated to the appendices.

---

1. I have been convinced by several of my non-engineer friends to put my "marvelous" discussion about electricity and how it works into the appendices. This causes me great personal anguish. I think I have written a clear, though somewhat shallow, dissertation on the subject. I believe that it is rather important to understand at least a little about electricity and how it works. I have been quite conscientious in trying to keep it simple. I have resisted putting equations into the discussion at all! Please try it. I hope you will like it.

Your Electric Bill

Your electric bill has a lot of information. In it you will find:

- your name and address
- your account number
- your meter number
- your meter readings for this month and last month. It will also
- translate the meter readings into energy, i.e., kilowatt-hours.

A watt is a unit of instantaneous power, i.e. a 100 watt light bulb uses power at the rate of 100 watts. If it is "on" for one hour it uses 100 watt-hours of energy or 0.1 kilowatt-hour (as we discussed in the introduction.) Therefore, you are "billed" for kilowatt-hours, or thousands of watt-hours by your utility company.

Your bill will have the charge for the kwh you used and usually a fuel cost is added to that. Sometimes there are other "adjustments," either plus or minus.

In a few parts of the country you will also be billed for the maximum or peak kilowatts, or demand (that lasts at least 15 minutes). This is a charge assessed by the utility company for using power. This charge is minimized by not turning all your appliances on at the same time. (All commercial accounts have demand charges which are based on their highest demand. Many utility companies remember, and continue to bill for, the highest demand for the period of a few months to over a year.)

An electrician friend worked with a man who lived in one of the areas that charge for residential demand. He designed and installed computer controllers in homes. These systems would limit the number of appliances in the home that could be turned on at one time, thus limiting the demand or kw charge. This is an effective means of controlling demand charges.

You may see the term "pcrf" on you bill. This is an abbreviation of "power cost recovery factor." This is the way some utilities recover their variable cost of fuel and the wholesale cost of energy they might have had to buy from other utility companies. Electric co-ops seldom generate their own power. They usually buy it from other utility companies. Co-ops frequently use the term "pca" which stands for "power cost adjustment." When the power cost is higher than expected, the cost is passed on to the customer through a positive pca. If the costs are lower than expected, the cost is passed on via a negative pca.

Analysis of your electric bills

One of the things you can and should do with your bill is to figure *your cost per kwh*. This is done by dividing the total cost by the total kwh of your bill. It will normally be in the range from 7 to 11 or 12 cents per kwh. Eight and one half cents per kwh is frequently thought of as "standard" whatever that might mean. Usually, however, your cost will be higher. (Large commercial customers can frequently negotiate a much more favorable rate because they use so much.)

If your cost per kwh never varies much over a period of a year or two, then it may not be important to plot your monthly usage. If it does vary a lot, like 30% or more, you should try to figure out why it varies. If it varies for no apparent reason you should contact your utility company and see if they can help you find out why it varies.

> Divide the total cost by the total kwh.

Some utility companies, such as TU Electric in Texas, include on each bill, a graphical summary of your last 13 months usage! This is useful in seeing patterns in your usage. You should do this even if your utility company doesn't do it for you. This can be done with a quadrille pad, one with little squares all over it. Draw a line across the bottom and label it with the month and year of each bill. Next, draw a vertical line on the left and able it with kwh. Make sure that your scale includes both your largest and smallest monthly kwhs. Then, plot two years or so of your past bills.

Some of the things your plot of consumption may show are:
* steady consumption throughout the year
* large fluctuations
* odd fluctuations.

If there is air conditioning in use, it will probably go up in the summer. If you have electric heat, it should also go up in the cold months. You should try to explain the fluctuations or non-fluctuations in terms of your usage. If you can not figure it out, call your utility company and ask for an explanation. There could be a billing error. If your utility company does not explain your billing history to your satisfaction, you may want to call in an energy consultant.

I have a chiropractor friend whose bills appeared to me to be in error. I examined his facility and figured out that even if he turned on every single electrical device in his whole building, he could not "pull" the demand kw for which he was being billed. We made an appointment with a utility representative. After some discussion, he agreed to have the meter re-calibrated. When they checked the meter, they found that it had malfunctioned. My friend got enough refunded to cover his electricity for about four months! It happens, so check it out—no one else will.

Air Conditioning & Heating

Now we can start on the point of the whole book—saving dollars and electricity. But let us first talk about what uses the most electricity. In this way we will know where our efforts can be most rewarding.

If you live in a hot climate, you will probably use more energy on cooling than any other one category. If you are unfortunate enough to have electric heating in a cold climate, you have the worst possibility. Next after these will be lighting, then comes everything else.

Air Conditioning

If you have air conditioning, this will be your largest cost when it's hot. Some of the things that can be done are listed here. First, if you are willing to endure some heat during hot weather, you can just about cut your bill in half by moving the thermostat from 72 to 78 degrees F. If the house is unoccupied during the day you *may* be able to save by changing the thermostat setting hotter during periods of no occupancy. This could be done manually or with one of the many inexpensive programmable thermostats. These programmable thermostats are relatively easy to install and operate. However, opinions are mixed about reducing costs. I have had an experienced air conditioning service man tell me that an even, constant temperature setting is not only better for the a/c unit but uses less electricity. I think it really depends on the individual circumstances.

If your central air conditioner is over ten years old, you might consider replacing it with a new, higher efficiency unit.[1] All electric appliances are now rated with an E.E.R. (Energy Efficiency Ratio) or S.E.E.R. (Seasonal Energy Efficiency Ratio). The

ANNUAL SAVINGS RESULTING FROM INCREASED ENERGY EFFICIENCY RATIOS ($/ton of air conditioning*)				
EER		Savings for (¢/kwh)		
From	To	7¢	8¢	9¢
6	7	$40	$46	$51
7	8	$30	$34	$39
8	9	$23	$26	$30
9	10	$19	$22	$24
10	11	$15	$17	$20
11	12	$13	$15	$16
12	13	$11	$12	$14
13	14	$9	$11	$12
14	15	$8	$9	$10
15	16	$7	$8	$9
*1 ton = 12,000 Btu per hour				

definitions are not important but knowing that higher numbers are better is the important thing. An efficient new central a/c unit should have an EER of 11 or higher. In humid climates, an extremely high EER, say 13 -14, might end up costing more to operate than the less efficient ones because to achieve the extreme EERs the designs may remove less humidity.

Comfort comes from having cool air at about 50% relative humidity. If the air is cool and the humidity is significantly higher that 50%, people feel

Comfort comes from having cool air at about 50% relative humidity.

1. Two speed a/c compressors are more efficient in use but cost more initially. Life cycle costs are less with these more efficient units.

"clammy" and tend to lower the thermostat setting. This, if it happens, effectively "undoes" much of the high efficiency by running the unit longer. See dehumidifiers below.

If you don't use all of your house on a regular basis, you can help by closing the a/c outlet vents in unused rooms and keeping those doors closed.

If you don't have central a/c, you may have window units. In principle, these should be more efficient, since they only cool where it is needed. However, they require more attention from the operator to achieve a significant reduction. Another factor is that window units cannot achieve the high EERs of central air units.

Furnace Filters

A dirty furnace filter can increase the cost of both heating and cooling by as much as 10%! That means that if your bill were $300, a dirty filter could cost $30 per month. Plus, a dirty filter will not clean the air as well. It really pays to keep your filters all clean. Replaceable filters are the simplest to manage. Just change them once a month when the unit is running. There are a multitude of longer lasting, cleanable filters. I'm sure that I could not endorse them all. Do be careful if you choose one of these because of the possibility of their being home to undesirable organisms. Whatever you choose, be sure that you get the best or near-best quality available—it will pay in the long run in comfort, health and dollars. Don't forget the air filters on your window air conditioners, either.

Condenser Coils on Air Conditioning Units, (& Refrigerators too)

The outside unit consists of a compressor, a fan and condenser coils to dissipate the heat that is "pumped" out by the a/c system. If the coils are dirty, as they surely get in a year of use, they need to be cleaned. Dirty coils do not transfer heat as efficiently as clean ones. This means that *your* unit has

A dirty filter could cost $30 per month.

to run longer to accomplish the same amount of cooling. You can clean them yourself by removing the covers of the unit. Be gentle. They are delicate. This doesn't mean they can't be cleaned, only you have to be gentle and careful. If you don't feel comfortable doing it yourself, get a seasonal checkup from a professional, and require that he clean them for you. The cost will be quickly recovered.

While you are at it, pull your refrigerator out and clean the coils on the back.

Ceiling Fans

The perceived "coolness" of the air depends on several factors. The temperature of the air is quite important. (Your nationality may also have an effect.)[1] To most people, humidity around 50% usually feels good. Of course, you remember that in the winter the weather forecasters frequently give the wind chill temperature. This lower temperature is based on the fact that air moving past the body "feels" cooler than it is. This fact is true in summer too. If the air is moving it feels cooler. Thus, ceiling fans can reduce your electric bills in the summer. By installing and using these fans, which use little energy, the perceived temperature will be lower and you can set the thermostat higher without your feeling hotter! Other fans may help reduce the perceived air temperature in other places too.

Evaporative Coolers

If you live in a dry climate, evaporative coolers might be an attractive option. This is because the only significant use of electricity is in moving the air, which is done by the blower. The blower will be somewhat bigger than one in a central air unit but

---

1. The air conditioning in the UN Building in NYC has requested thermostat settings from 62 to 88 degrees F. depending on the nationality of the tenants.

use far less energy than the compressor, its fan and the inside fan that are all required for central air.

Passive Approaches to Cooling

Other things you can do to significantly reduce the cost of air conditioning are to:
* use awnings to shade windows and even west walls,
* apply heat reflecting window coatings, and
* use landscaping to shade the house, especially the south and west walls. Ideally, plant deciduous trees that lose their leaves in winter because the heat of the sun can get through the branches in the winter when the heat is desirable.

Air Leaks in your House

Some experts claim that, in a house that is not well-sealed, air leaks may be a major source of conditioned air (hot or cold) loss. These leaks can add significantly to the cost of maintaining any desired temperature. You need to:
* Ensure that the opening into the attic is airtight.
* Seal/caulk around doors and windows on the outside of your home.
* Remove switch and outlet plates. Install foam seals under them to prevent conditioned air from getting into the walls and out of the house.
* Check for air leakage along bottoms and tops of all walls and corners.

If the attic is properly sealed, and its ventilation vents are open, as they should be, one or more thermostatically-controlled roof exhaust fans will reduce the temperature in the attic tens of degrees. However, if the opening to the attic from the house is not well-sealed, it will cool the attic even more — by "sucking" cooled air out of the house into the attic!

When you heat with electricity, you pay for several times as much heat as you actually get.

Air Conditioning and Heat Pump Cycles

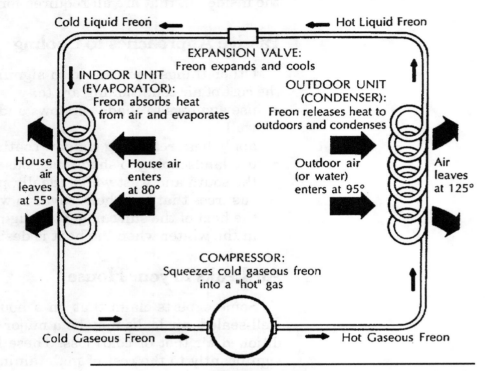

The refrigeration cycle in the summer cooling mode.

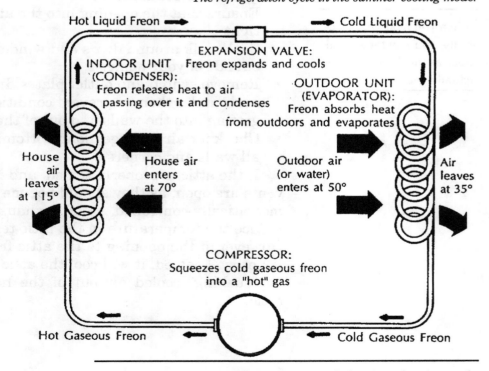

The heat pump cycle in winter heating mode.

Heating

Heating will only have a noticeable effect on your electric bill if you use and pay for electric heating. The reason that electric heating is so expensive is that electricity started out, in most cases, as fossil fuel, coal, oil or natural gas. The fuel was burned and turned into heat. The heat was then transformed into electricity. This transformation—from heat to electricity—is very inefficient. So when you heat with electricity, you pay for several times as much heat as you actually get.

The most economical forms of heating are, first, natural gas or coal (if that is abundant where you live). Next comes Liquid Petroleum Gas (LPG), sometimes called propane or butane. If your only alternative is electricity, then a heat pump is next best. See the previous page for the diagrams. A heat pump is an air conditioner that can reverse the coolant flow. Thus, in the summer, it pumps heat from the inside to the outside cooling the house. In the winter, it pumps heat from the outside to the inside warming the house. Because the coolant starts to freeze between 30 and 40 degrees, heat pumps experience a transition to pure electric heat below this temperature. And last, of course, is pure electric heating, which—in almost all cases—is the most expensive form of heating, especially when life cycle costs are considered.

There is a device that eases the burden of electric heating called an electric thermal storage unit. This device senses the outside temperature; and if the temperature is cold, it heats ceramic bricks to about 1400°F during the night when electric rates are lowest. Then, later in the day, when the electric rates are highest, it releases it stored heat to the living space by circulating inside air over the hot bricks. Steibel Eltron[1] makes a nifty line of these units as do other companies. Ask about them. Price range is $700-$1500. Where needed, they will pay for themselves in a year or two.

---

1. Steibel Eltron, P.O. Box 40, Tioga Center, NY 13845, 800-582-8421

Heat Pumps

Heat pumps are devices that pump heat! (Isn't that remarkable?) An air conditioner is a type of heat pump, in that it "pumps" heat from the inside of the house to the outside. Since that is all that an air conditioner does, it is not usually called a heat pump. That term is usually reserved for devices that can "pump" heat from the outside to the inside of your home. There are many kinds of heat pumps. An air conditioner that can reverse its coolant flow is called a heat pump since it can move heat or "cool" either way—from the inside out or the outside in! This type heat pump is an "air-to-air" heat pump (my terminology as far as I know. I haven't heard it used by others.)

There are also heat pumps that will take the heat from the inside of your house in the summer and put it into (heat) your swimming pool. This same device can pump heat from your pool in winter, if it is not too cold—like freezing, into your house.

Geothermal heat pumps are ones which "pump" heat from or into the earth. We will discuss these in more detail later.

Passive Heating

The possibilities of passive heating, absorbing the sun's energy to heat your home, are manifold. The details are described in several good books. The essentials include:
- landscaping,
- house orientation relative to the sun,
- properly designed overhangs of the roof,
- lots of glass on the south side,
- heat storage material in the house, and a
- house designed for natural convection heat distribution.

If you are interested in finding out more, visit your local library or call Real Goods.[1]

---

1. Real Goods,966 Mazzoni St., Ukiah, CA 95482. (800) 762-7325.

Insulation

Insulation is "measured" in terms of "R-factor" or resistance to heat flow ratings. For example, a six inch layer of fiberglas has a rating of R-19. The larger the R- rating, the more resistance to heat flow and the better the insulating effect. Most insulated houses have a higher R- rating in their ceilings than in their walls. This is because the major source of heat flow in is usually through the ceiling. Next come the walls, and then probably, but not necessarily, the floor. If you live in a building with a concrete slab floor, there is not much you can control.[1]

If you own your house or condo, you should determine how well it is insulated. Most insulation companies will come to your house and evaluate its insulation without cost or obligation. Insulation options[2] might include fiberglass, either in batts or "blown-in," cellulose fiber and certain kinds of foam. You should probably do some research beyond talking to insulation contractors before deciding for yourself. If you are a do-it-yourselfer, you could probably install it yourself.

Mobile homes need "skirts" that prevent free air movement under them to be properly insulated. If air is allowed to move unrestricted under the floors it will increase undesirable heat flow, i.e., "in" in summer and "out" in winter. The same is true for homes that are built on pier and posts. In these cases, there may be a real need to insulate your floor from underneath.

---

1. Install wall to wall carpeting over a thick closed cell foam pad if you believe the floor to be a significant source heat gain or loss.
2. There are some health hazards with some kinds of insulation. For example, when polyurethane foam burns, it produces toxic fumes! There is controversy over whether fiberglass presents any real health hazard. It probably does but that has not been "proven" yet.

Thermostats

Newer thermostats are simply more accurate and respond faster to the environment. Older thermostats registered temperatures accurately enough, but would activate the heat or air within a broad range, a few degrees. New thermostats read more accurately and turn on the units with less swing in range. Many people, however, don't believe thermostats, preferring to use them as some sort of catchup device. Don't keep changing it. Find the right level and leave it. If you still have a problem with comfort, the problem lies elsewhere. Look at heat pipes, duct blowers, vent closers and other solutions.

Humidity and Water Vapor

When houses are built now, the outside of the wooden frame is usually covered with an insulation board that has a metal foil covering. The metal foil fills two purposes: it improves insulation[1] and it also acts as a "vapor barrier." Water vapor or humidity moves through the walls of your house as if they were not there! If your home has been exposed to high humidity for some time, the walls floors and ceilings may literally contain several thousands of pounds of water.

Water vapor or humidity must be controlled for comfort. A relative humidity[2] of about 50% is most comfortable for most people at "room" temperature. In the winter, when temperatures are really cold, there is very little water in the outside air. So, when that air is heated in the house, it is extremely dry. For this reason humidifiers are often installed in the heating systems in houses in cold climates.

---

1. Radiant heat shield.
2. Relative humidity is the percent of water vapor in the air compared to how much it could hold if it were saturated, i.e., 100%. The *amount* of water vapor air can hold (100%) varies with temperature, i.e., warm air holds much more water vapor than cold air.

In humid climates, dehumidifiers may be an economical step to improved comfort and reduced cooling bills. In commercial buildings, the air conditioning systems often cool the air far below the comfort zone to reduce its humidity. Then the "too-cool" air must be reheated from its very cold 100% humidity condition to "room" temperature with about 50% relative humidity. There is now a more economical approach for both commercial buildings and home owners.

Heat Pipe

Heat pipe from Heat Pipe Technology, Inc.

Heat pipes advanced from a laboratory curiosity to a useful device when NASA applied the technology to the temperature control of spacecraft. A heat pipe is a sealed, tubular, passive device that absorbs heat from one end and gives it up at the other end! A passive device is one that requires no input of outside energy. The tube contains a quantity of coolant which will change from liquid to gaseous state at the temperatures of interest or application. The tube also contains a wick which will absorb the liquid coolant and, through the mechanism of surface tension, "wick" the liquid to the other end of the tube.

The principal of operation is as follows. As the liquid coolant absorbs heat at the "cool" end, it evaporates into the gaseous state. In doing this it absorbs the heat of evaporation. The now gaseous coolant migrates to the other end of the tube where the gas pressure is less. In this environment, the gaseous coolant condenses and returns to the liquid state, giving up the heat of evaporation it received at the other end. This makes this end "hot" now. The condensed liquid is absorbed by the wick and transported to the cool end again! This cycle goes on continuously as long as there is a temperature differential between the tube ends. The temperatures must be above the freezing point of the coolant and below the boiling point of the coolant so that the state changes from liquid to gas can take place. No energy input is required if the heat transfer at the ends is through the mechanism of radiation. In an air conditioner, it does take some energy to blow the air over the heat pipe device.

A very smart young man by the name of Khanh Dinh licensed this technology from NASA and adapted it to the dehumidification of air conditioned air. As air conditioners in humid climates cool the air and reduce the air temperature, the air cools to the dew point, or 100% humidity (Rh). At this point humidity will be condensed out (that is the reason your air conditioner in your house has a water drain pipe). However, under these conditions the air coming from the cooler is at nearly 100% humidity, which is not comfortable. When the air leaves the register, it mixes with room air and warms up from Rh = 100% to Rh = 70-90%. As a result, you will probably turn the thermostat down so that the humidity of the air is more comfortable, but of course, the air is also colder (up goes the electricity bill).

The heat pipe as adapted by Mr. Kanh is installed in the air conditioning ducts on either side of the evaporator, or cooling coils. The "hot" return air is first passed through the cooling part of the heat pipe. This results in a "precooling" of the warm air going into the air conditioner. Since the air conditioner is cooling already cooled air, it cools it even colder, thus forcing additional humidity out of the cooled air. This supercooled air leaves the cooling coils colder and drier than it would have been without the precooling part of the heat pipe. The heat extracted from the warm air by the heat pipe is then "piped" in the gaseous state to the warming part of the heat pipe. The heat pipe coolant condenses and releases the heat it picked up from the incoming air into the supercooled air coming from the air conditioner, thus heating it to about the temperature it would have been if the were no heat pipe. Since this is a very low loss process requiring no external energy input, there is nearly no cost of operation. (The fan blowing the air through the cooling coils will have to blow the air through three cooling coils instead of one but that is almost insignificant.)

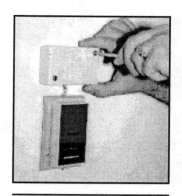

ThermoRider — an easy to install solution to high electric bill

These devices are not cheap to install but have a very long, maintenance-free life. The cost recovery should be estimated on the basis of a 15% to 25% reduction in electrical cooling costs. The company has multiple offices through out the country, at least in the humid parts.[1]

ThermoRider™

A second way exists to condition air more efficiently, whether you have new or old units. If you have a standard air conditioning or heating system, not window units, you may be able to shave up to thirty per cent off the bill. How? ThermoRider.[2] This clever device is simple in concept. It can significantly improve the efficiency in most air conditioning systems. When the air conditioner is normally

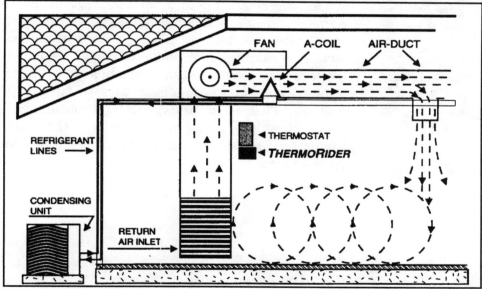

Your Air conditioning system with ThermoRider.

turned off by the thermostat, a full charge of compressed, cooled freon remains, along with all the

1. Contact Heat Pipe Technology, Inc., P.O. Box 999, or 803 North East Street, Alachua, FL 32615, Phone (800) 393-3464.
2. ThermoRiders are not widely known. For more information, call (713) 787-9910 or write ThermoRider, Inc., 6060 Richmond #305, Houston, Texas 77057.

cool air in the ducts. This cooling "power" remains even after the a/c is shut off by the thermostat and is effectively "dumped" without producing cooling. A ThermoRider keeps the evaporator fan running for a few minutes extra. The result is the extraction of the "cooling" that would otherwise be lost and that you have already paid for!

It is a proven device: post office installations in Houston have shown an average savings around 30%. The ThermoRider may be removed easily and taken along if the owner moves.

I have had a ThermoRider in my home for two years and am very satisfied with the resulting savings.

Automation

An interesting catalog of automation devices for homes and small businesses comes with Windows-compatible software. This software allows the owner to manage the usage of devices such as controllers and automated switches for lights, a/c, appliances and motion detectors to turn lights on and off. This is an inexpensive grouping of products.[1] Now let's move on to lighting, the next most important area for understanding and reducing your electric bills.

---

1. Home Automation Systems, Inc. Costa Mesa, California 92626. Phone: (714) 708-0610

Lighting

Lighting accounts for 20 to 25% percent of the electricity sold in the United States. A portion of the lighting is incandescent, a portion fluorescent and a small portion sodium, mercury vapor and other variants. Looking at some of the facts of lighting, we find that a great deal can be done to improve the lighting efficiency nationwide and, in most cases, in the lighting right around us. How much do you know about lighting?

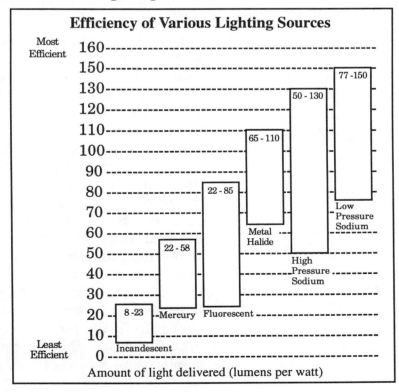

Efficiency of Various Lighting Sources

Most Efficient

160
150
130
120
110
100
90
80
70
60
50
40
30
20
10
0

Least Efficient

77 - 150 — Low Pressure Sodium

50 - 130 — High Pressure Sodium

65 - 110 — Metal Halide

22 - 85 — Fluorescent

22 - 58 — Mercury

8 - 23 — Incandescent

Amount of light delivered (lumens per watt)

Incandescent bulbs function with about 6% efficiency; therefore, about 94% of an incandescent bulb's output is heat. Here are some other facts:

- To light an incandescent bulb for its lifetime, some 736 pounds of coal must be burned to generate enough electricity.
- A compact fluorescent will only consume 177 pounds of coal and last many times longer than incandescent bulbs.

Of what importance are these two facts and figures to you and your future lighting needs? Industry and government looked into this question recently and wrote the Energy Act of 1992, also known as EPACT.

EPACT (Energy Policy Act of 1992)

Congress recognized that most lighting purchased in the U.S. continued to be the cheaper, low efficiency type. Since that contributed to environmental problems by its squandering of resources, Congress passed the Energy Policy Act of 1992. Called EPACT, it mandated new efficiency standards for lamps and fixtures and set a deadline for manufacturers to bring their products into compliance. The law directly applies to popular fluorescent sizes and to reflector incandescent lamps. The question that we all ask is, "Can we and should we accept this new concept that lighting efficiency is more important than light bulb cost?"

The answer is "Yes." First, we must stop thinking of lighting as just an overhead expense, pun aside. It is not a fixed, immutable expense.

As of October 31, 1995, EPACT has been fully implemented for lighting. The law provides for substantial fines for anyone making or distributing non-compliant lamps in the U.S., including foreign-made lamps.

On incandescent lamps, bulbs made for both European and domestic markets must be universal socket to fit the larger European 220 volt use, then retrofitted for the narrower 120 volt American application. By looking at the base of the bulb, you

> ...most lighting purchased in the U.S. continued to be the cheaper, low-efficiency type.

> Lighting efficiency is more important than light bulb cost.

can tell if it is a larger non-domestic glass bulb rather than the slimmer American variety. The glass made for the European bulb has a larger base so the American version will not be as secure and may loosen and stick in the fixture. Additionally, the domestic bulbs give more light for the money; they are brighter.

Replace incandescent bulbs with compact fluorescents.

Wherever possible, we should replace incandescent bulbs with compact fluorescents in the fixtures used most often and that have the highest wattage bulbs, if the replacements improve or maintain the quality of life and reduce expenses. Security and outdoor lighting fall into this category, as do kitchen lighting, garage lighting, staircase lighting and so forth.

There are really two ways of measuring light. One is the *quality* of light from non-sunlight sources (bulbs) and the inability of artificial light to cause colors to appear as they would in sunlight. The other is the *quantity* of light, measured in lumens, which is a measure of the intensity.

It is possible for a fewer lumens of light of high quality color to be as comfortable to "see in" as more lumens of lower quality color. (Please read this sentence again and make sure you understand it. It is important!) Let us now explore the nature of light in more detail.

Light Color

If you have ever seen light separated by a prism into its beautiful and rich component wavelengths and colors, you know that white light is really a mixture of colors. Your ability to distinguish colors (preference) is unique to you but closely parallel other people's preferences. Historically, we are a race of beings who have been sitting around campfires and fireplaces for centuries. We spent the majority of our waking time in daylight. Color preference is built into us.

You can find a color chart in the appendix to explain this subject more completely, but, essentially the higher the *color temperature*, the bluer the

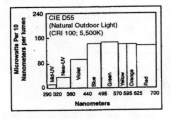

Color of Daylight

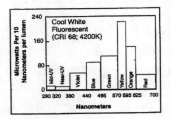

Color of Cool White

light. The lower the temperature, the redder the light. Color is measured in degrees Kelvin (°K), with daylight about 5,500 degrees Kelvin, light from incandescents around 3,000 degrees.

While color temperature has no relation to room temperature, visually perceived warmth or coolness is a psychological effect of low or high color temperature lighting.

When we consider improvements in lighting, cost savings improve as a side benefit. Quality of life should be the most important aspect of all this. Safety, health, comfort — these come first. Savings are incidental (but real).

Color Rendering Index

Another measure of light quality, called CRI or *Color Rendering Index*, ranges from zero to 100. This scale measures the ability of light to render an object's true color when compared to daylight. 100 is perfect, 0 absolute darkness. The reference point of all lamps with color temperature lower than 5000° is a theoretical black body, absorbing light rather than emitting it. Higher color temperatures than 5000° (such as Vita-Lites) would use natural daylight as a reference point.

The CRI is fast becoming the standard to use. Fluorescents with a CRI of 82 or higher are exempt from EPACT regulations as Congress recognized lamps with high CRI's to be of superior light quality.

LIGHT, COLOR RENDERING INDEX & COLOR TEMPERATURE		
Light Source	CRI	Degrees Kelvin
Natural Daylight	100	5500 - 6500
Incandescent	90	2700
Cool White (fluorescent)	62	4100
Vita-Lite (fluorescent)	91	5500
Compact Fluorescent	80	2700

Incandescent Light

Incandescent bulbs, you may recall, were invented by Thomas Edison after experimenting with more than ten thousand different filaments. Incandescent bulbs tend to give off a yellowish color of light, typically 2700° Kelvin. The range is from 9,000° Kelvin (blue light) to 1500° Kelvin (orange-red). Daylight is 5500 to 6000° Kelvin or more. Firelight, candlelight and tungsten bulbs will give off more reddish light than daylight. Look at a lamplight in a room during the day and you will see how the light is yellowish, or take a photograph in lamplight and see how everything is reddish. Thomas Edison was interested in creating light. He did not care how much energy it used or how white the color. *Now* we care. We have options because of him, but we have more and different options than he had.

Why would you want his incandescent light? Well, it is better than no light at all and it seems natural at night, when we cannot compare it to daylight. But remember this: mankind spent thousands of years around campfires and this color light seems right to us at night. That is why fluorescent light seems unnatural to us at night. It *is* unnatural to us. The color violates thousands of years of culture. Remember this when selecting nighttime lighting. Incandescent light is also readily available and cheap. Incandescents lose light temperature or turn redder as they age and lose intensity as they approach burn out; about 25% of output is lost by the end.

Incandescent lights are really burning filaments. New technology makes it possible to generate light without the same burning filament, or with filaments that burn more slowly. Thus were *energy-saving bulbs* created. A 52-watt energy-saving bulb may not put out quite as much light as a 60-watt incandescent, but it will use less electricity and will last longer, all things considered.

There are also long-life bulbs. These have a heavier filament, and consequently do not burn out as fast — they may last 5000 hours. The down side is that they are even less efficient than regular

Thomas Edison was interested in creating light. He did not care how much energy it used.

incandescent bulbs and can cost more to operate. They have a lower temperature light and produce fewer lumens per watt. Energy-conscious people will only want to use these in locations where changing a bulb is difficult or inconvenient.

There is also an inexpensive device that looks like a coin and fits in the light bulb socket under the light bulb. One type uses a diode to reduce the energy consumed by the bulb. The output of lumens is reduced substantially. A 100 watt bulb will consume about 60 watts but emit the equivalent of a 40 watt bulb. The efficiency is also reduced, but the *life* is extended by as much as a factor of 50! Another type uses a thermistor which reduces the light output and efficiency by 10% but extends the life by a factor of three.

Fluorescent lighting

Fluorescent lamps convert electricity into visible light up to five times more efficiently than incandescent lamps. They last up to 20 times longer, too. Generally, most of us think of long tubes of sick-colored light when fluorescent is mentioned. The term itself means "glow" or "fluoresce." Energy flows through gas and causes it to release electrons which impact the material on the inside of the tube causing it to produce visible light.

New developments allowed new designs, so let's first talk about *compact* fluorescents. These bulbs will fit into regular incandescent light sockets. Some of them take a moment or two to light up fully but usually give more natural coloration. Remember, the chief advantage is that they give the same amount of light at a fraction of the cost of operation.

They initially cost more than an incandescent bulb, but they will last longer and use less electricity. Typically, they will last ten or more times longer than the comparable incandescent! Fluorescents will produce the same level of light for only one-

Long-life bulbs are less efficient than regular incandescents.

Same amount of light at a fraction of the cost of operation.

fourth of the energy of their incandescent counterparts.

LIFETIMES OF LIGHTS IN HOURS	
Standard Incandescents	1,000
Long-life Incandescents	3,000
Halogens	2,250
Compact Fluorescents	10,000
LUMENS PER WATT	
Incandescents	16
Compact Fluorescents	60

Compact fluorescents in high-use areas give the greatest monthly savings because their use saves changing bulbs and yields the greatest environmental benefits.

Amory Lovins of the Rocky Mountain Institute concluded that replacing a single 75-watt incandescent light bulb with a compact 18-watt fluorescent (which lasts 13 times as long):

- reduces emissions from a coal plant of up to 2,000 pounds of carbon dioxide and 20 pounds of sulfur dioxide (which causes acid rain).

Where are these lights best suited? Everywhere at home! And also where they will remain on awhile, four hours or more at a time. They may deteriorate faster at low power, so they should not be used with dimmers. They are great in table lamps, stair wells and hallway lights but the bulb length can be up to 7" which may restrict usage in enclosed fixtures. Duro-Test markets a 20 watt Tri-Power-Twist compact fluorescent. This bulb is manufactured in Korea, is 6.9" long and comes in both incandescent-simulating and sunlight-simulating colors. Most compact fluorescents have a rated life of 10,000 hours or more.

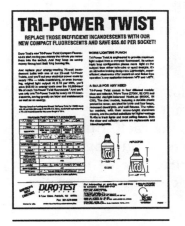

Duro-Test's Tri-Power Twist compact fluorescent bulbs.

If they are to be outside, choose an outside-rated bulb. Otherwise, they will not provide much light when the temperature drops below 40°F. Look at a *Phillips Earthlight Electronic Energy-Saving Bulb (Outdoor):* it says it is equivalent to the light output of a 75-watt incandescent bulb.[1] It generates 1100 lumens, using only 18 watts! The manufacturer says it lasts 10,000 hours. If you pay $22.95 retail for this bulb, it will cost more than the thirteen 75-watt bulbs it will replace. But you will not have to get up on a ladder as often and unscrew all the other protective stuff on your fixture; you won't have to buy a big box of 75-watt bulbs at the hardware store and store them for ages (and the cheap ones don't last as long); and you will probably save about $57.00 over its lifetime[2] — despite the cheaper incandescent bulbs — because of the lower energy costs! If you can afford the greater initial cost, it is usually a better buy and you can afford lunch at an expensive restaurant as your reward, or shoes for the kids, or some other such thing as you desire or need.

If you need DC compact fluorescents, you can get them in 12, 24, 36 or 48 volts DC rated at 100,000 hours. These are 85% efficient at 12 volts, 13 watts and 100% output.[3]

Fluorescent Tube Lighting

We haven't discussed long tube fluorescent lamps yet. You probably don't have any in your home unless you put them in yourself. Builders seldom go to the extra expense of putting in much higher cost fluorescent fixtures for $15-$30 each when they can install incandescent fixtures for a

---

1. Philips Lighting Company, 200 Franklin Square Drive, Somerset, NJ 08875-6800. Assembled in Mexico. Box made from recycled paperboard.
2. Life cycle costs again.
3. S&H Alternative Energy Products available from Alternative Energy Engineering (800) 777-6609, Fowler Solar Electric (800) 914-4131 and Sunelco (800) 338-6844.

buck or so. This is probably mostly due to the competition in the building industry. However, you should know about several new developments so that you can, if you wish, install them in your present home or specify them for a new home being built for you.

As you may know, three principal parts make up fluorescent tube light fixtures: the tubes, the ballast and the fixture itself. You may choose among many fluorescent tubes. You used to be able to find 48 inch tubes built in Mexico for less than a dollar which are rated at 40 watts like standard tubes which cost $2-$4 each. The cheap tubes don't last as long and give lower temperature light. A better buy is the 34 watt cool white or a 34 watt variation of the cool whites. These lamps meet the minimum standards required by EPACT. They provide a 15% reduction in energy consumption when operated on a ballast rated for 34 watt lamps. And then there are the tubes which produce light with a much higher CRI. These will provide a better light for working or reading but their cost is even higher that the standard tubes.

Special tubes that generate no light but draw little or no power entered the market under the term *phantom* tubes. A fixture with one working tube and one phantom tube operates some 40% cooler than otherwise with two fluorescent tubes (and remember that empty ballasts still draw power). Payback, they claim, is within one year and 100% return on investment every year thereafter. The power factor increases with this type of system so actual savings may tip 70% in some locales and situations.[1]

Another option is really high quality fluorescent lamps, such as those made by DuroTest.[2] They make a variety of energy-saving, excellent light quality lamps. These range from high brightness T-10 lamps (85 CRI) to full spectrum fluorescents (96 CRI). For example, two of their Aurora T-10 4 foot

> Phantom tubes operate cooler ... payback in one year ... 100% ROI every year thereafter.

---

1. Development Sciences, Inc.
2. DuroTest Lighting, 9 Law Drive, Fairfield NJ 07004, (800) 289-3876.

tubes can replace 4 conventional Cool White T-12 tubes in a fluorescent tube fixture and produce almost the same amount of perceived light. They have an expected life of 24,000 hours. These tubes stay brighter longer too, along with a much higher CRI and they work with either magnetic or electronic ballasts. Duro-Test says that an additional 30 watt savings is achieved when two of their new Ultra-9 lamps are used with an electronic ballast. Over the rated life of 24,000 hours, you can save $275 for each fixture.

Duro-Test also manufactures the Vita-Lite fluorescent, the world's only patented general purpose full-spectrum fluorescent lamp. It provides the necessary wavelengths that sunlight contains which contribute to our general heath and well-being. It is used in light therapy to treat "winter depression." Humans possess two areas of ultraviolet sensors: the eyes and the skin. Based on recent scientific and medical studies, we need at least moderate exposure to the complete spectrum of natural light in order to function at optimal levels. Our internal clocks are regulated by sunlight! Full-spectrum daylight also regulates our endocrine system and our immune system. Our proper bone growth is regulated by the light.

Vita-Lites are so close to natural sunlight that they can fool animals. Many bird and reptile breeders use these lamps to increase the quantity of offspring when housing their animals indoors. Several years ago, the Bronx zoo installed full-spectrum fluorescents as nighttime security lighting. An unexpected effect occurred. Many of the zoo residents gave birth over the winter instead of spring. It seems that the animals perceived the days to be longer and thought winter was over.

Acrylic Light Polarizing Panels

Most old fluorescent fixtures shine through standard prismatic panels mounted under the lights. The polarizing panel improves the effectiveness of the light by "veiling" reflections. Read that as reduc-

Save $275 for each fixture.

Vita-Lite ... full-spectrum fluorescent lamp.

Breeders use these lamps to increase offspring.

ing glare. Color improvement may be evident. This style of lighting also reduces eye fatigue and increases visual comfort! How does this panel save money? By producing more detail visually than higher levels of conventional fluorescent light, this panel substitutes light *quality* for light *quantity*, a very inexpensive solution to savings and comfort.

Ballasts

All fluorescents require *ballasts* to convert the house power to the form of electricity needed by the fluorescent lamps. The ballast regulates the voltage and current. Typically, each type of bulb requires a specific type of ballast.

Core-coil or magnetic ballasts, electromagnetic in nature, have driven fluorescent lights since the beginning. They frequently produce abundant noise in addition to light; the noise comes as a sixty cycle hum which can be quite annoying. Tubes powered by this type of ballast frequently flicker at sixty cycles per second. Many people notice this with considerable annoyance. The "standard" grade ballast costs $15-$20 and has a reasonable probability of failing before too long. A good rule of thumb: avoid any ballast that specifies "For Residential Use Only."

Higher cost ballasts are more efficient and last longer. Extreme efficiency ballasts dissipate less of the energy and last even longer. Electronic ballasts, on the other hand, with solid-state technology, weigh less, run the bulbs silently at higher frequencies, and cost more in general. Electronic ballasts can also dim fluorescent tubes so that they produce less light and use less energy too.

"A fluorescent lamp ballast serves two primary functions: it provides the high initial voltage necessary to start the lamp, and it regulates current during lamp operation. The ballast also may provide voltage to heat the lamp's electrodes to assist in lamp starting or lamp operation.

Magnetic ballasts contain a magnetic core of several laminated steel plates wrapped with aluminum or copper windings. Older magnetic bal-

lasts require as much as 16 watts to operate two 40-W T-12 lamps (total 96 W). Such high-loss ballasts can no longer be sold in the United States for commercial purposes. Instead energy-efficient magnetic ballasts are available that use high-grade materials and require approximately 8 W to operate two 40-W T-12 lamps (total 88 W).

Cathode-disconnect ballasts are magnetic ballasts that do not provide voltage to heat the lamp electrodes during lamp operation. This saves 6 to 8 W (total 80 to 82 W) compared with an energy-efficient magnetic ballast. NLPIP published a Specifier Report on cathode-disconnect ballasts in 1993.

Electronic ballasts regulate voltage using solid-state components rather than a magnetic core. The products that NLPIP tested operate lamps at high frequencies, ranging from 19 to 46 kilohertz (kHz). High-frequency operation increases the efficacy of the lamps by 10 to 12%, compared with conventional 60-Hz operation of magnetic ballasts. For example, an electronic ballast operating two 40-W T-12 lamps can use as little as 72 watts total (an 18% reduction compared with an energy-efficient magnetic ballast), while reducing light output only slightly. In addition to the reduced power requirements, most electronic ballasts offer several other advantages over magnetic ballasts: reduced flicker, reduced noise, reduced heat output, ability to operate up to four lamps and reduced weight."[1]

Some people don't like fluorescents at all. Core-coil ballasts flicker when starting. They run at 60 cycles per second and bother some people. Electronic ballasts have a 10,000 hour life but they run the bulb at 30,000 cycles per second, so the flicker is not apparent.

A solid-state electronic ballast designed by the Lawrence Berkeley Laboratory of the University of California and the U. S. Department of Energy uses 30% less power than standard ballasts. That is 60

---

1. *Electronic Ballasts*, National Lighting Product Information Program, Specifier Reports Abstract, Rensselaer Polytechnic Institute, Volume 2 Number 3 May 1994.

watts nominal input with 100 watts nominal output. Magic! This ballast works more efficiently than even high-frequency electronic ballasts.

Extreme efficiency ballasts are also available, too.[1] Genlyte of Garland makes high efficiency ballasts. Ballasts usually last several times as long as fluorescent tubes. They do fail, however. Consider higher efficiency replacements for failed ballasts.

Finally, on the subject of ballasts — they consume energy even if a tube is 'burned-out.' In fact, they consume some power even if the tubes are removed! So if you have fluorescent tube fixtures, make sure that the switch is turned off. And tell your boss at work too!

Energy-saving conversion units are available in many places, DuroTest to name one. You might hear this as a retrofit. DuroTest provides a 2 for 4 retrofit, or delamping. Using Aurora T-10's, a retrofit can save 96 watts per fixture. See the table below which shows how much you can save per 4 lamp fixture.

kWh rate	5 days/wk 12 months	6 days/wk 12 months	7 days/wk 12 months	24,000 hours Bulb life
$0.05	$44.93	$53.91	$62.90	$115.20
$0.06	53.91	64.70	75.48	138.24
$0.07	62.90	75.48	88.06	161.28
$0.08	71.88	86.26	100.64	184.32
$0.09	80.87	97.04	113.22	207.36
$0.10	89.86	107.83	125.80	230.40
$0.11	98.84	118.61	138.38	253.44
$0.12	107.83	129.39	150.96	276.48
$0.13	116.81	140.18	163.54	299.52
$0.14	125.80	150.96	176.12	322.56
$0.15	134.78	161.74	188.70	345.80

1. Genlyte Controls, Garland, Texas. (214) 840-1640.

These units change out easily. Disconnect the ballast. If they are in an older building, leave the extra ballast. For $1 per year, they offer insurance if the other ballast fails.

Neodymium Lamps

Incandescent neodymium lamps use neodymium oxide that filters out excess yellow in the spectrum of the filament, generating daylight-balanced light as it is normally perceived from natural sunlight. Colors do look alive with this bulb, which the manufacturers say lasts up to 3,500 hours. This light dresses up artworks, displays, homes, clothing, food. Relatively expensive, it lasts several times longer but if you like color, this is really nice to use. Many people feel better with this light around them. This lamp is substantially more expensive than conventional incandescent lamps. Bulbrite Industries, Inc.[1] makes a bulb like this in Korea.

Most Neodymium lights are manufactured in the far East. Imported incandescent lamps have a history of unreliability and poor performance in North America. Pet shops that sell the neodymium lamps as basking lights cite early burnout as a major complaint. Duro-Test manufactures a line of U.S. made neodymium lamps which the company guarantees for one year. The Neo-white lamps emit 20% less infrared energy and are therefore 20% cooler than standard lamps.

Exit Lights

If you live in an apartment house or condominium, you will encounter exit lights. Almost all businesses use them as required by various laws and codes. Most of these lights reside in little metal boxes with a little 25-watt light bulb. Switch to any of a variety of 12-watt compact fluorescents. These will last some two to five times as long and use less energy than incandescents. Even better, switch to a

1. BULBRITE Industries, Inc. 71 Schrieffer St., So. Hackensack, NJ 07606 (201) 489-7777.

new fixture using LED (light emitting diodes) that barely consumes any power.

DuroTest makes a retrofit kit for exit signs, converting them to LED exit signs. They claim that the original incandescent signs use 40-50 watts versus the LED at 1.8 watts, or 9-26 watts for fluorescents. Figures show the operating costs to be low, around $1.50 per year compared to the $35 of an incandescent fixture! Service life: 80-100 years (estimated). No maintenance and always lighted during emergency, this kit will meet government safety guidelines. If you have an exit fixture anywhere, look at this kit.[1]

"Most internally illuminated exit signs use incandescent lamps, which consume approximately 24 to 40 watts (W) per sign, or up to 350 kilowatt-hours (kWh) of electricity per year. Exit signs that use more energy-efficient light sources and retrofit kits for converting signs offer the potential for energy savings. However, signs using energy-efficient light sources can vary widely in power characteristics, visibility, and readability. NLPIP produced Specifier Reports: Exit Signs to identify performance concerns and help specifiers select products that save energy and can be seen in clear-air and smoke conditions."[2]

Halogens

Consider halogen bulbs to be "turbocharged" incandescents. They are 10 to 15% more efficient than incandescents but they cost more because the filament is housed in a chamber filled with halogen gases (chlorine, etc.). When the bulb heats up, the particles lost from the filament get recycled from the gas back onto the filament and thus it lasts longer. They are sensitive to operating voltage and should be used usually at maximum output to work properly.

---

1. DuroTest Lighting, 9 Law Drive, Fairfield, NJ 07004 (800) 289-3876.
2. *Specifier Reports: Exit Signs*, National Lighting Product, Information Program, November 1994.

If you have 75-watt floods on the porch, driveway or garden, consider switching to halogen bulbs. The extra heat that halogens generate will not affect you at all in these applications but a 45-watt halogen will give off as much light as a 75-watt floodlight. They also last much longer so if they cost a little more, they will be worth it in two ways: longer life and lower operating cost. But the most important consideration is understanding your usage and selecting the one that achieves what you want in *quality*.

These bulbs put out very white light. Automobile headlights are often halogens. As a side effect of this bright white light, they give off a lot of heat, too. Halogens are good for reading, sewing, hobbies, that sort of thing. Write down the wattage of the bulbs you are currently using. Replace them with equivalent *lumens*, not wattage.

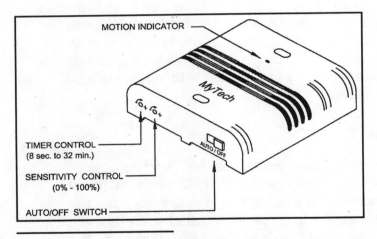

Occupancy detector from MyTech Corporation.

Occupancy Detectors

We all know that lighting may not be needed in some areas all of the time. We've seen downtown skyscrapers lighted up at night when the cleaning crews are around and we know that one floor at a time might be more efficient, don't we? The same is true at home.

We can turn off the lights or we can install occupancy sensors. If you live alone, you probably don't need these but they are a great convenience. If you have children or handicapped folks, though, the sensors are really nice. No more shouting, "Turn off the lights!" across the house. The lights just turn off by themselves when you leave, or when the kids leave. One particularly nice application is in entranceways and driveways: when you drive up, the light turns on in front of the car or on the porch or at the back door where you will be entering. Convenient and safe — a nice combination. The Real Goods Catalog[1] lists a motion-activated, solar-powered security light for $139. Also listed: an energy efficient nightlight and wall switch that fits into a standard rocker switch plate, using only 2¢ per year, they claim. Price: $27.00.[2] They show another simple night light for $9.00 or three for $24.00.

Genlyte and others make devices to turn off lights in any room not occupied after an adjustable time delay. The switches and detectors have an infrared or heat detector which looks for movement. If the detector senses no movement after the set delay, it turns off the lights. Some variations also turn lights on when a the room is entered, while others require a switch to be turned on.[3]

Seventh Generation[4] sells a nightlight called Nightguide that senses motion and responds with a bright light that stays on for any time you specify (5 seconds to 15 minutes after motion stops). The price as of this writing: $32.00. This is a lot for a nightlight but not much for safety and convenience. This is one on which I won't calculate savings on. If it saves one battered, bruised shin and stubbed toe, it is worth it if you can afford it!

However, we will look at the expense of an occupancy sensor put out by MYTECH.[5] This ultrasonic sensor, called Supra Sensor, detects changes in movement rather than body heat. It is sensitive enough to detect a hand movement while other types may require body movement to activate. This sensor can work in bathrooms, bedrooms, indeed throughout the house. (They also work very well in commercial applications such as locker rooms, restaurants, classrooms, offices and hotel rooms.) Percentages saved will vary but ranged generally from

---

1. Real Goods Catalog, (800) 762-7325.
2. Ibid., Real Goods Catalog.
3. Ibid, Genlyte.
4. Seventh Generation® Products For A Healthy Planet, 1 Mill St., Box A-26 Burlington, VT 05401 (800) 456-1177.
5. MYTECH, 706 Brentwood St, Austin, Texas 78752-4042 (512) 450-1100.

15% to 69%. This line of products is manufactured in the USA.

Timers

Timers work well in many applications. These are usually very inexpensive. Real Goods Catalog lists a light-sensitive sensor socket timer for $19.00. They describe it as "...an innovative way to reduce your electric bill with a built-in photo eye that automatically turns a light on at dusk and turns it off six hours later." An electrician can quote you the cost of rewiring all or part of your house. You can buy the parts in advance and have them wired by professionals. The cost per hour then is nominal. Remember to evaluate this cost against the long-term cost of the old style you are using, and factor safety and convenience as well into the equation. You will never regret this change if you can afford it or complete it.

Other sensors include computer-controlled boxes such as Home Automations Systems markets for your home PC for only $49.95.[1]

Dimmers

Dimmers, simple and useful, can be used in many areas of the home to reduce the lighting level when high levels are not required. Not so good for halogens, the dimmer's lower voltage tends to shorten the life. However, if dimmers are used with halogens, the bulbs should occasionally be turned on high. This reverses the decomposition, somewhat, we are told by a manufacturer.

Green Lights Program

The EPA created a Green Lights Program to encourage energy conservation through innovative allies. The EPA can supply you with a directory of the allies committed to providing energy efficient

1. Home Automation Systems, Inc., 151 Kalmus Dr, Costa Mesa, CA 92626. (800) 762-7846.

alternatives as well as free information about these products.

Conclusion

We have talked about a *lot* of things about lighting. There is a lot to understand if you want to make some real improvements in this area. The "best" was presented first — compact fluorescent screw-in replacements to replace incandescent lamps. Most of the rest has more or less to do with the *quality* of the light in your home. The quality issue may well apply to your business or job also.

If you need help visualizing the changes you can make, *Real Goods Trading Corporation* — the world's largest distributor of low-energy lighting— sells ***The Book of Light*** which contains an immense hoard of information about efficient lighting. It even has cutouts of the various screw-in replacement bulbs so that you can be sure the light will fit your fixture.[1]

SAVINGS OF COMPACT FLUORESCENTS V. INCANDESCENTS		
	Phillips SLS 20W	75 Watt Incandescent
Cost	$30.00	$0.50
Expected Life	5 Years	160 Days
Annual Usage in Watts	20	75
Cost of Energy	$4.50	$16.50
Bulbs Replaced in 5 Years	None	10
Total Expense	$48	$88
Lifetime Savings	$30+	

What can we glean from all this information? See the chart above. First, cheapest is not always

1. The company can be reached at (800) 762-7325 or by writing to Real Goods Trading Corporation, 966 Mazzoni Street, Ukiah, California 95482.

the least expensive. Second, light quality and emotional context may be altered by lighting. Preference is important, regardless of cost. Third, selecting the best of the options for the purpose will probably save energy and money in the long run. Choose the light that you want and that you need for your purpose, then select the best quality you can buy. It will pay handsomely.

Saving With Appliances

We can understand and reduce our electric bill further by considering appliances where much of our consumption originates.

In a home survey, completing a list like the one in the appendix will acknowledge whatever electrical items you actually have and use. We recommend the survey for several reasons: to know what you have and to know the real impact of the appliances on your bill. This surveying — for most of us just one hour of work — will be worth at least $300 per year, maybe much more, so just gird up and do the survey. If you save each year for twelve years the way you should this next year, you will be able to save at least $3,600, and maybe more, without further work. That money would make someone happy. Give it to your spouse, your church, your charity, your kids or grandkids, your employees, beggars, brokers, bankers or yourself, but don't throw it away. With the motivation speech now completed, let's move on to details.

Energy Guide Labels

With the survey, you will know what to compare when you replace existing items. From Chapter 1, you already know your cost per kwh. You will know what the operating costs will be, versus your current appliance. When replacing an old appliance or buying an additional appliance, buy the most energy-efficient version you can afford. Why?

Because appliances use hundreds, if not thousands, of dollars of electricity during their lifetime. Sometimes a higher priced product will start saving money immediately and cover the cost difference in the first month or two. This is especially true for air conditioners and other high consumption items. For example, a window air conditioning unit $30 cheaper with a much lower efficiency may use $100 more of electricity the very first month!

Since 1980, Energy Guide Labels have been required on furnaces, refrigerators, freezers, water heaters, clothes washers, dishwashers and room air conditioners. They are not used on many other appliances.

These seven types of major appliances represent 73% of all home electric consumption. The large number in the center represents the average electricity rate and the cost of its use with this appliance for a year. If it has a number rather than a cost figure, it represents a ratio of values: energy efficiency ratio (EER) or seasonal energy efficiency ratio (SEER). Minimum efficiency standards took effect in 1987 and change periodically. Once again, a more expensive model may be far cheaper in the long run. Take ten years as the operating life of the appliance. The annual operating cost figure on the label multiplied by ten gives you a total operating cost for that product. Add the initial cost of buying the item and you have the total cost. Do this for all the options you are considering to really compare the prices.[1]

Cost of Appliance from store
+ operating cost x 10 years
(or more) equals total cost

---

1. Incidentally, I am still using a refrigerator (in the garage) that we purchased when my forty-year-old son was about two. It was a high-priced unit then. However, I might save money over the next ten years if I trashed it and got a more efficient one.

Using the survey form in the back of the book will help you go through this sort of inventory and analysis in your home. For now, let's just talk about the way to look at each item.

By appliance, we mean refrigerators, ovens and products of that sort. As far as electricity consumption is concerned, a computer or printer, drill or sander will be no different than a refrigerator or stove. (You won't hear that sentence in many other contexts.)

Let's look at the larger categories first, then the specific devices that make up the categories. Let's include the standard items like kitchen appliances, then add an increasingly common category in the home — computers, printers and the like, and regular entertainment devices like televisions, stereos and such, and finish off with shop appliances such as saws, drills, motors, pumps, sump pumps and so forth.

Refrigerators and Freezers

The largest household consumer, other than air conditioning, comes from the refrigerator and freezer (which are also a form of air conditioning too.) These appliances can be a large part of your home electric bill, particularly if the unit is old and inefficient. Coupled with an old freezer, an old refrigerator can really drive a bill up fast.

The number one way to utilize your appliance effectively: set the temperature controls correctly. That means don't set the temperature level lower than you need it to preserve food. My refrigerator has a setting for temperature as well as season! Thus, I have to set it differently in the summer than in the winter. Buy a refrigerator or freezer thermometer to find out what the real temperature is in your appliances, both day and night. Adjust it appropriately. Don't overload these appliances. The air must be able to circulate to keep the contents cool. Naturally, don't hold the doors open too much either. To check the door seals, take a dollar bill and close the door on it. Pull the bill out. If it comes out easily, you probably need a new door gasket. Do this for the freezer, too, if it has a separate door.[1] Then if you have external condensers and coils, clean them.[2] All those dust bunnies eat electricity. The transfer surfaces should be clean and free of gunk. Consider an energy-efficient unit.

Facts:
- Running two units cost much more than running one larger unit (Oops, I already admitted I run two [blush]).
- *Side by side* models use 35% more electricity than *freezer on top* models.
- Chest freezers run more efficiently as a rule than uprights.
- Automatic defrost units consume as much as 40% more energy to run.

Stoves, Ovens and Ranges

In England, quite often the same stove that is used for cooking is also used to heat the house. Water heats continuously in this same stove. The oven is always warm and the stove top ready to use. This sort of usage is not common in the United States.

We tend to buy appliances for very specific purposes. The efficiency improves by correct selection and usage of the appliances. For example, let's say we have an electric range in the kitchen. Improper use will create extra heat that has to be remedied by more air-conditioning or ventilation. Thus, we should use the equipment only when necessary. Turn on each burner only as needed. Match utensils

1. If you don't have separate doors for your refrigerator/freezer, you probably would save money in the long run by replacing it. Horizontal door models usually run more efficiently than the vertical side-by-side varieties.
2. Many recent refrigerators use the outside walls of the unit to replace condenser coils. There will always be a fan near the compressor. This area will need cleaning for maximum efficiency.

and equipment to the job you're doing. Use a small pot on a small burner. Use the time selectors and computerized aids if you have them. Consider using other appliances when practical. Convection ovens, toasters, infrared fryers, microwave ovens—all these are more efficient forms of cooking.

Proper ventilation and exhaust systems help a lot, though many older homes do not have exhaust vents and other fancy things.

Facts:

- Small appliances use less energy to cook than larger ones.
- Bake several items at a time. Do NOT preheat oven. Turn the oven off 5 to 10 minutes before removing food.
- Use the same size pot as burner.
- If you buy a gas range, buy one with electric ignition (saves heat generation from the pilot light and the gas itself).

At a rural electric co-op trade show recently, *flash ovens* debuted. They use less power than conventional ovens and cook much faster. They are just now available commercially. Look at these remarkable appliances if you have the chance. Ask about them if you are building a new house or remodeling.

Dishwashers

New dishwashers test the water temperature so that the properly heated water from the hot water system doesn't get heated more electrically by a booster. If the water is hot enough, it is used right away. Only if it needs heating does the dishwasher turn on additional capabilities. Great use of technology! This feature does not require human input. So many devices are really too complicated for us to set, much less remember how to use.

The DOE concluded that handwashing dishes may be more energy *inefficient* than using the appliance, particularly when full loads are utilized. The DOE also suggested the booster heater option, which they calculate to cost about $30 additional on new appliances. This surcharge can be expected to pay for itself in one year or less. The DOE also found that the most efficient dishwasher on the market can cost half as much to operate as the most inefficient model!

Facts of Interest:

• Efficient dishwashers may use less energy than handwashing.

• Appliances with booster heaters save money in most applications, though you should turn down the water heater temperature for maximum savings.

• For greatest drying efficiency, use air dry cycles if you are not in a hurry.

Clothes Washers and Dryers

Clothes washers function much the same way as dishwashers. A deluxe model may have features that will pay for themselves early on. Light wash sessions, light drying, timed drying, drying by sensors that work just long enough to give the proper humidity in the exhaust air, timed usage for off-peak rates or for stored-energy usage.

Suggestions:

• Buy machines that allow control of water temperature and level.

• Buy dryers that allow moisture sensing, cool down cycles and, if gas, electric ignition.

• Wash and dry full loads.

• Use cold water as much as possible.

• Do not overdry clothes.

Hot Water Heaters

Insulate your older electric hot water heater[1] with a inexpensive jacket available at hardware stores everywhere. Also insulate your hot water pipes going into the house! Very cheap foam insulation is easy to buy, easy to install and easy to pay for.

---

1. Gas hot water heaters are difficult to insulate safely. Know what you are doing before you try it or get professional help.

Water heaters come with adjustable temperature settings. Some of the new ones allow travel settings as well as temperature choices. The Department of Energy[1] recommends 120°F for most households, if your dishwasher booster heats the water further, but some dishwasher detergent formulations only work at 140°F or more. At that temperature, scalding can occur so be careful in choosing your water temperature. Each ten degree change can alter your energy consumption for that task by 3 to 5%.

Some utility companies allow off-peak control devices that shut off water heating during peak demand periods and offer a financial incentive to choose this option. Check with your local utility company.

Fix all water leaks and bad washers and seats, pipe joints and shower heads. They can penalize you significant dollar amounts each month. We suggest that you also consider the installation of water-saving low-flow shower heads which cut water usage to 2-3 gallons per minute from the 5 or so typically used. Finally, drain your hot water heater periodically to eliminate sediment which inhibits heat transfer from the coils. Every six months is not too often.

Free Hot Water

Several methods emerged to generate free hot water as a by-product of other functions. Generally, these processes are not solar. We cover solar energy in a special chapter for those interested.

Hot Water Generated by Air Conditioner Heat

Since you have read this far, we know that you just finished reading about the hot water heaters. A

1. U. S. Department of Energy by the National Renewable Energy Laboratory DOE/GO-10095-063, PS 204, January 1995 available through the Energy Efficiency and Renewable Energy Clearinghouse operated by NCI information Systems.

company called Heat Pipe Technology, Inc. markets a product called *The Hot Plate*™ as "free water heating for your home."

They describe the product as:

"a revolutionary heat recovery unit which captures waste heat created by air conditioners."

"...It can provide all the hot water needed for a family of four during the cooling season, and saving up to two-thirds of the power used in winter if installed with a heat pump. It fits under the hot water tank and uses no other space. It requires no pumps or sophisticated controls, is self-regulating with no moving parts and no electrical input."

They claim that it transfers wasted heat from the air conditioner to the hot water tank, heating the water up to 140° F. Furthermore, it lowers operating and condensing temperatures of the air conditioner, reducing even the cost of that operating system somewhat.

Distilled Water

Distilled water replaces bottled water and purifies even the most despicable sources. Pure Water, Inc., invented a way to distill water with your power source (electricity, gas, propane, butane, solar, diesel motor-generated) and use the waste heat to heat enough hot water for your family's daily use. Distilling water uses a lot of energy, as those of you with chemistry class backgrounds already know. Distilling water removes chemical contaminants, bacteria and the like from a poor water source. This concept embodies *smart kilowatt hours*. It can be programmed to use off-peak or odd hour electricity. The hot water in the heater for household bathing and washing comes from the initial steps to distill the water for drinking. This device is worth a look if you want or need distilled water.[1]

---

1. Pure Water, Inc. 3725 Touzalin Ave., P O Box 83226, Lincoln, Nebraska 68501 (800) 875-5915

Small or Hand Appliances

You won't likely walk away while forgetting to turn off a hair dryer because it makes so much noise, but you may walk away without turning off coffee pots, waffle irons, steam irons, soldering irons, televisions, stereos, video games and all sorts of household electrical devices. As a side-bar, coffee is better brewed and stored in a thermos than dehydrating on the coffeemaker into a witch's brew. It is not nice to nag, but let's agree that 200 million people using lots of items each day needlessly will waste a lot of power and natural resources needlessly. It may not impact your bill but for future generations, turn off unused appliances. There. It is out of the way now.

New Appliances for Pets

We might as well tell you about some of the new appliances available since we have your attention. Most of you have pets — dogs and cats. We found several pet-related products that don't use much power but will greatly increase your peace of mind and the quality of life for your pets at least. One of the gadgets is an electromagnetic cat or small dog door opener. Your pet wears a small magnetic key on the collar which opens the door only for your animal. You can set it for two way entry, entry only, exit only or locked. It keeps strays and wild animals out. Great idea — about $70. Also, look at the automatic pet feeder if you have to travel a lot, and the motion sensor animal alarm to stop animals from invading your lawn or garden. Both are about $60. We found them through Home Automation Systems[1] out of Costa Mesa, California but others are surely available.

---

1. Home Automation Systems, Inc. 151 Kalmus Dr., Suite L-4, Costa Mesa, California 92626. (800) 762-7846.

Wood-Burning Appliances

Many information sources will tell you how to use these devices. Secondary only to safety, the level of efficiency should be the top consideration in choosing a wood-burning stove or appliance.

According to a National Association of Home Builders survey, most buyers want a fireplace. However, a fireplace can actually result in heat loss from the home. Necessity aside, esthetics make a fireplace desirable (that quality of life factor again). If you want or have a fireplace, consider improving its efficiency.

EFFICIENCY OF WOOD-BURNING APPLIANCES	
Open masonry	10% to 20%
Masonry w/ steel shell circulating fireplace	10% to 20%
Masonry fireplace w/ inserts	10% to 50%
Heat-storing fireplaces/masonry stoves	20% to 60%
Open door stoves/Franklin stoves	30% to 45%
Circulating stove	40% to 50%
High efficiency non-acrylic stoves	60% to 70%
Catalytic	65% to 75%

Office Equipment

Half the homes in America have computers and printers. These produce heat to increase the air conditioning load. Many computers and printers now come with energy saving options. Buy those if possible. When your office will be unoccupied, turn off the computers and printers, especially on weekends or when you go away.

If you can afford these items, and you like gadgets, consider a home management system. We are told that some thirty-five million computers are not actively used a majority of the time they are running. The EPA instituted an Energy Star™ program which partners with the computer industry to promote energy-efficient computers and peripherals. Companies that participate design devices that shut down partially or completely when not being used. Savings can be 50 to 75%. An EPA Energy Star™ logo will identify compliance.

Meters

Texas Meter & Device Co. offers metering devices for home users, although their base is industry. You can buy a reconditioned meter for as low as $25. Both primary and secondary meters can be acquired. Why? To check the meter you have or to sub-meter a mobile home, piece of equipment or shop, curiosity, a lot of reasons. Just thought you ought to know how to get a meter if you want or need one.[1]

---

1. Texas Meter & Device Co., P. Box 3088, 1509 New
   Dallas Highway, Waco, Texas 76707, (817) 799-0261.

Solar Heating, Water Conservation and Other Tidbits

Solar energy comes from the sun. Every day we get a new batch of energy for the earth; we get so much energy each day that if we were able to "capture" *all* that comes to us, in just one day, we could meet the energy needs of the whole planet for about two years.

Both renewable and free, solar energy may be harnessed for heating water, heating and cooling the home, generating electricity which can power appliances, automobiles and lights. We will discuss both solar hot water heating and solar home heating in this chapter. For the generation of solar-generated electricity itself, please read the following chapter entitled *Living off the Grid*.

Solar Heating

Solar heating represents a viable option in many parts of the country. Solar heating will not affect your electric bill if you heat with gas. It will, of course, reduce your gas bill and be much kinder to our environment.

Of course, there is a cost of converting to solar heating or installing the initial equipment. After installation, however, it is essentially *free!* In most parts of the U.S. today, we have enough solar energy to supply at least 75% of all heating requirements. Thus, solar heating exemplifies a truly practical thing to do almost everywhere.

Solar energy-harnessing devices typically embody either solar panels or solar water heating schemes. Solar hot water heating in the U.S. dates back a long way: photographs taken in 1922 portray the manufacturing of solar hot water heating panels!

To convert a non-solar heated home, we must add a supplemental solar-heated hot water system. Although this may require an investment of a thousand or two dollars, operating and maintenance costs will be negligible for a *long time* into the future. Consider expanding the system to whole-home heating, or at least supplemental heating. Building a home with solar hot water or a complete solar heating system installed is not much more expensive in most places. Shop around, call or write one of the associations listed in the appendix to get a list of the approved installers in your area.

Solar Water Heating

This method of heating water, like the Hot Plate™ technology using air conditioner waste heat which we examined earlier, utilizes freely available energy but requires a modest investment. While we could find only one type of hot plate technology, we found that several solar water heating systems exist.

In the very simplest, water circulates by gravity as it is heated. Called a *passive system*, with no moving parts, it is quite reliable. Place some hot water tanks in the sun, usually on the roof, paint them black and take the hot water from the top where it is the hottest. It's a little more complicated than that but it is simple in concept and implementation.

Active systems circulate the water through the solar heating panels. In locations where freezing might occur, the outside part absorbing solar heat must use a fluid that will not freeze. This heated fluid is pumped through a heat exchanger to heat the water in the house.

Solar water heaters may be either passive or simple active types. The heart of the system, the solar heating panel itself, can be homemade or purchased commercially. Homemade ones perform adequately and are much less expensive. The straightforward plumbing requires only a knowledge of how to run water lines.

Since solar heating is not normally available at night, a 24-hour supply of water must be stored during the heating hours of the day. This will require a substantially larger hot water storage tank. Since the quantity of hot water available varies due to weather, an auxiliary water heating capability is highly desirable. The plumbing for hot water on the house side of the hot water heater would not need to be changed. (This is true of all types of solar water heating systems.)

The direct water heating active systems, suitable for locations that don't freeze, are little different except that they have forced circulation of the water and do not require that parts of the system to be located in the attic. Cold weather systems become much more complex. The fluid heated in the solar panels cannot be mixed with consumable or potable water. It is *not* good to drink! So you have the added complexity of a heat exchanger, another circulation pump or two and other components.

Of course, once installed, the system and all your hot water are almost free of out-of-pocket expense.

Before you install one of these systems, you should learn a great deal more. Become your own expert by talking with your local plumbing contractors, contacting you city, county or state energy conservation departments or agencies, reading the most recent books on the subject and, if you are so inclined, "surfing the net" in search of the best and latest information.

Consider adding extra insulation around your existing hot water storage tank, even if you do not install a solar hot water system. Electric hot water heaters can be quickly, easily and inexpensively insulated. Gas hot water heaters are much more complicated to insulate because of the need for unrestrained flow of combustion air and exhaust products.

In conclusion, solar water heating is a viable option for most parts of the U.S. A solar water heating system will take some time, money and effort to implement, an expense or investment offset by significant future savings.

Whole House Solar Heating

Heating the whole house with solar energy is also practical for most parts of the country. This approach can include a variety of approaches beyond the solar panels — sun spaces, landscaping and house orientation are all factors to be considered.

In most existing solar heated homes, the solar heating system supplies only 75-85% of their heating needs. The rest is supplied by some more conventional form of supplemental heating.

Let's talk about each component of the home heating system in turn. First, the hot water heating system or solar panels. For whole house heating more solar panels will be required than just for domestic hot water. The panels are usually located on the roof of the house. However, they can be on the side of a nearby hill on the ground near the house or almost any place else you might find convenient. "Nearby" is the operative word here. Running hot and cold water lines for a quarter or half mile will *not* improve the system cost or performance! Several solar panels will be required. As you become an expert, you will find out how to calculate the number needed. Unless you want to set up a factory, you will probably opt for commercially manufactured units rather than homemade. The pumps, storage tanks and other components will probably be purchased from commercial sources anyway.

Sunspaces, parts of a home that face south, have lots of glass. They have overhangs or eaves to let the winter sun shine into the house to warm it and prevent the summer sun from shining inside much at all. This results, of course, from the sun being high on the horizon in the summer and much lower in the winter. In fact, the farther north you are located the more pronounced this factor becomes. Also, the sunspaces optimally include many large heat storing objects such as metal 55 gallon drums full of water painted black and sitting where the sun shines most of the winter day. Brick or other masonry walls and floors are also good heat storage devices. Sunspaces should also have vents and windows arranged so that natural convection can circulate the collected heat through the rest of the house.

A solar heated house would also include much attention to the complete insulation and sealing of the entire house. Most of the existing solar heated homes are not "over" large, economizing on space as well as everything else. This is, of course, only personal preference.

Landscaping would ideally include deciduous trees on the south and west to block the summer sun and evergreens on the north to block cold north winds. This is an obvious over-simplification but landscaping is highly personal and far from any area of expertise which I might lay claim to. Site layout is another important factor upon which I cannot really instruct.

Water Pasteurizers

Solar-powered water pasteurizers may clear the water for people in remote areas or where contaminated water causes disease. The SolSaver™ pasteurizer requires no fuel or electricity and uses thermal activity rather than pumps to move the water. Water coming in flows through copper tubing to a collector for heating. This solar collector will not allow the dispensing valve to open until the water reaches the necessary temperature. Called the SolSaver™, this device implements the findings of biologist Robert Metcalf of California State University. He discovered that most microbes and biological or disease-causing water contaminants die at temperatures below boiling. John Grandinetti of Grand Solar, Inc.[1] pursued this line of inquiry and devised a way to heat water to 80°C and kill most of the common problem bacteria. For example, *Onchocerca volvulos* (the worm causing river blindness) dies above 131°F (55°C); Hepatitis A dies above 149°F (65°C); *E. Coli*, cholera and polio perish at 140°F (60°C). We ran across information on this invention from The Rotarian Magazine in an article by Nancy Chege, who saw it in World Watch magazine and reprinted it.

If you have gone to all the trouble of building a solar heating system or water pasteurizer or any other system, don't overtax it by wasting hot (or cold) water. Thus we shall discuss water conservation.

Water Conservation

Another concept appropriate to discuss at this point is the conservation of water, both hot and cold. Since our ground water requires energy to "purify" and provide at house pressures, saving water saves energy. Reducing the consumption of hot water will save additional energy. Not only are water bills often high, but widespread water shortages occur periodically. We seem to be using it faster than nature will put it back. Let's look at an item of great interest to people in remote locations or places with contaminated water.

Probably the easiest and simplest way to conserve water, both hot and cold, is to use a low-flow shower head. You can test your present shower head with a gallon bucket. Turn on your shower full blast and see how long it takes to collect a gallon of water. Twenty seconds for a gallon means you have a high, 5 gpm flow shower head. You can replace it for $10-$30 with a low flow device. Actually, the low flow

1. Grand Solar, Inc., 2169 Kauhana St., Honolulu, HI 96816. (808) 737-3536.

shower heads feel about the same in the shower as the high flow ones but use much less water. If you are concerned about how it might feel, be sure you can return the low flow if you don't like it. Then try another.

The simplest approach is to reduce the *amount* of hot water used. This can be done by installing low flow shower heads and bubblers on every faucet indoors. Also, only run the dishwasher and washing machine when full loads can be washed. A water faucet dripping one drip per second wastes about a $1 per month. It can be fixed in a very short time and with minimal cost.

If you don't have them already, install "bubblers" on every water outlet in your house except your bathtub.

Reducing Electric Costs If You Have an Electric Hot Water Heater

Find out if your utility company gives a rate break to heat your hot water in "off" hours. If they do, install a timer to heat your water before 6 or 7 AM, whenever the rate goes up. If they don't give you a rate break, forget the timer. However, if they bill you for demand, you should use the timer to preclude everything running at once which will "max-out" your demand charge.

Insulate your electric hot water heater. Your heater has some insulation under the metal outside cover. However, this insulation still permits substantial heat loss from the hot water over time. When the water cools, the heater reheats it. Insulating your tank substantially reduces the reheating required. Kits are available from hardware and building supply stores. The costs ranges from around $10 to $40, instructions included. Gas hot water heaters are *much more difficult* to insulate. They require proper air flow to and from the combustion area or there is a risk of fire and/or explosion.

Wireless Solar Lighting

Comtrad Industries[1] markets a wireless line of products. One is a solar sensor for security using quartz halogen bulbs with built-in heat and motion sensors. The light mounts anywhere. Solar panels mount on your roof. Here is a product that adds convenience and safety with little negative impact.

They also produce lighting for gardens, pathways and other outdoor lighting. These units do not attach to solar panels. They are wireless and utilize fluorescent technology and last about six hours after dark. You don't pay for operating this outdoor lighting.

More Information on Solar Energy and Equipment

If this subject excites you, or if you are going to build a new home soon, look in your library for a copy of *Solar Journal* or order it for about $25 a year.[2] The industry is rapidly heating up as designers and users learn that it is easy to incorporate solar energy these days into homes and business and the costs have dropped dramatically while dependability improved.

We suggest also that you look in your yellow pages, particularly in big cities, under Solar Energy Dealers, Solar Energy Equipment and Systems (Manufacturers and Distributors), Solar Energy Equipment and Systems (Parts and Supplies), Solar Energy Equipment and Systems (Repair and Service) and even Solar Energy Research and Development for firms engaged in the business. Since the field is changing so fast, keep an open mind.

---

1. Comtrad Industries, 2820 Waterford Lake Dr #106, Midlothian, Virgina 23113. (800) 992-2966.
2. Solar Industry Journal/Solar Industries Association, 122 C Street, NW, 4th Floor, Washington, DC 20001. Phone (202) 383-2670

Off the Grid

Home Power Magazine.

Really *Alternate* Life Styles

In this great US of A, several thousand homes, by choice or location, do not connect to any utility company's *grid*.[1] Living off the grid, now an economically feasible alternative, usually costs more than buying power from a utility company. However, if your home or homesite sits some distance from the grid, off-the-grid living may be the lowest cost method of electricfying your home. Even if you live in town, you may not want to deal with the power company! Or you may want to really get "even" and sell your excess electrical energy back to the Utility—they *have* to buy it from you! Many remote commercial applications can benefit from photovoltaic systems at significant savings and quite a few residential setups can justify the initial expense.

Today we have several ways to live off the grid: two principal renewable energy sources do not involve a utility company — photovoltaic conversion

---

1. The term "grid" refers to the distribution system used by utility companies. It includes the high voltage towers for long distance transmission. It also includes the power poles around town with transformers on them. For areas with under ground electric service it includes the underground wires and transformers. Essentially, every thing from your meter to all the generating facilities inter connected with your utility company.

of the sun's energy directly to electrical energy and windmills or wind turbines which convert the energy of the wind into electrical energy. Additional alternatives such as water-generated power exist but solar and wind systems cost the least and remain the most popular. Popularity reduces the cost of these systems. Additionally, the newest area of interest, geothermal, offers astounding capabilities for heat pump utilization.

Off the Grid

Independent power providers, also known in the trade as IPP's, have been looking at this alternative. Some utility companies such as Edison will hand a list of providers to a customer wishing to take advantage of the utility company's financing on an uneconomical line extension. Then the customer and the provider take it to the utility company for approval. Now not only large customers but also homeowners can talk with their utility companies for the latest information. The homeowner may be able to live off the grid without significant expense. After all, the object of the homeowner will be to get off the grid, not necessarily to sell excess energy back to the utility company.

New technology now allows residential cogeneration controlled by your heating thermostat and a diesel engine using only ½ gallon of fuel oil per hour. Not cheap, though, at around $8,000.[1]

Easy Information

We highly recommend the purchase of *Home Power*'s CD-ROM for researching this subject easily.[2]

Anyone interested in this subject should also be on a computer linking to the internet. Many sources

Home Power's CD-ROM.

---

1. Intelligen™ Energy Systems, Inc., 98 South St., Hopkinton, MA 01748. (508) 435-9007.
2. Home Power, P. O. Box 520, Ashland, OR 97520. (916) 475-0830.

are springing up on the net and they are far too numerous to mention.

The Photovoltaic Cell

The thought of living *without* electricity is not very appealing to most folk, but using it from a renewable resource, such as the sun or wind, might be very appealing to many and a necessity for quite a few. With the advent of the semiconductor and the transistor came the discovery of the photovoltaic cell, a specialized semiconductor device that generates a small DC voltage when exposed to the rays of the sun. Technology increased the output, made them weather resistant and long-lasting.[1] Several companies now sell *arrays* of these cells. The arrays connect to a controller which funnels the energy in excess of what your are using to batteries. The batteries store electrical energy for your use when the sun is not shining. If necessary or desired, this DC power can be input to a solid state inverter which changes DC to AC. In this way you can power refrigerators, stoves, food dehydrators, pumps, hot tubs, TVs, computers and any other devices you can't live without.

Off Of (But Connected To) The Grid

The control system will also interface with the grid. In the event you need more energy than you can collect, you can use some from the local power company! The really great part is that if you produce more than you need the utility company is required to *buy* it from you!

---

1. Present, commercially available devices should last decades. Some of the early units used on satellites are still "ticking" after more than 20 years.

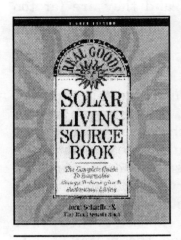

Solar Living Source Book.

Again, if you are going to invest several thousands of dollars in such a system, you *need* to become your own expert. Get a copy of the *Solar Living Source Book.*[1] After you have become familiar with it, get and read several of the books they sell. Talk to the suppliers they recommend. Once you know enough to know what you really want, then start designing and acquiring. Real Goods offers technical support and actual design services from *real* experts. We found a number of designers of solar electric water pumping systems for livestock and homes.[2]

Wind Turbines

Windmills have evolved a long way from the metal towers with the many bladed fan and regulating "tail" that pumped water in the old days. Windmills of today are called *wind turbines*, and are in use domestically and commercially, generating power, sometimes in competition with the utility companies. The machines of today use highly refined turbine technology to extract the maximum amount of energy from wind of nearly any speed. They do have maximum wind speeds; they will shut themselves down so that they do not self-destruct from over-speeding. They are exceptionally simple and quite reliable.

Popular Science ran a comprehensive article on wind power.[3] The cost of wind-generated power has now crossed over the oil and gas-generated costs but has not yet coincided with coal's cost yet. Projections show that by the year 2010 the wind-generated prices will be the lowest of all.

1. From the Real Goods Trading Corporation, 966 Mazzoni Street, Ukiah, CA 95482-3471. (800) 762-7325.
2. Aurora Power & Design, 3412 N. St., Boise, ID 83703. (208) 368-0947.
3. Popular Science, July, 1995: *The Forecast for Wind Power,* Dawn Stover.

Several utility companies throughout the world install wind turbine systems for their remote customers. Many more are considering doing this.

In fact, if you live more than a half mile from a utility line and have a prevailing wind of around 10 miles per hour, it will be cheaper to install a wind turbine than to connect to the power lines of the utility!

You need to be an expert before investing in today's wind turbines. Real Goods has lots of information on these also. If you are seriously considering wind turbines, get a really good book or two, such as Paul Gipes' *Wind Power for Home & Business,* available from Real Goods. Either photovoltaics (PV) or windmills, or both in combination, can meet the energy needs of most households. This approach implies that you, as the homeowner, have given much thought to efficiency in all aspects of energy usage. Most household devices are available in low voltage DC form now to work with these systems.

Geothermal

We mentioned geothermal applications in detail earlier in the heating and air conditioning segment. Geothermal can mean several things: getting hot water from the ground (Old Faithful at Yellowstone) or now simply using the earth as a heat sink or source. The temperature of the earth a few (5-15) feet down is a constant 55°F all year long, everywhere (almost). So you can pump heat from your house to the earth in summer and pump heat from the earth to your house in winter! The efficiency of these systems is high. They are *most* beneficial in extreme climates, hot or cold. The earth loop can be vertical holes or loops of flexible pipe laid out overlapping and flat and covered with several feet of earth.

The Geothermal Heat Pump Consortium just approved grants to three pilot geothermal heat pump marketing programs. One of the programs will allow the co-op to experiment with a loop-lease program which enables homeowners to lease ground loops for geothermal heap pump systems for only $15 a month! Each home would use ground loops requiring four 125 foot vertical holes. [1]

1. Electric Co-op Today. (703) 907-5583.

What Utility Companies Are Doing

The big boys are slugging it out over the changes to come this decade in the industry. The main issues emerging are safety, profitability and capacity. Utility company programs involving public education and innovative research with understandable applications make television news and newspaper headlines frequently.

Many issues confront the power industry today. The effects of high voltage magnetic fields on people and animals, nuclear power, national power distribution, rural electrification, water-generated power and many other areas now reach public debate and interest. The futures exchanges now trade energy futures which include gas, heating oil, crude oil and electricity. Even little issues and small moves in commodity markets grab the attention of power companies.

Quality of Life Issues

One such subject: security lights. Security lights make us feel safer but generate lots of light to cloud up the night sky. Many utility companies are aggressively moving to outlaw mercury vapor lamps which put a third of their light upwards. The companies also require shielding on other outdoor lamps. High pressure sodium lamps with the pinkish tone must be fully shielded and low pressure amber lights partially shielded.

Benefits of all this ordinance-passing: clear and visible night sky, lower cost of operation. The light shielding programs build good images for utility companies and provide enhanced productivity for all of us.

Safety

Many companies now purchase television time to show tips on energy conservation and high power line safety. Image and perception play important roles in legislative and consumer issues. In times past, utilities did not have to worry about your opinions but with competition looming and high costs for electricity, consumers want to hear something, if brief, in the way of feedback. Safety is a safe issue to build image and community awareness. Most utility companies and certainly the majority of rural co-ops now interact well with communities. Utilize their speaker services, their inspection services, their publications.

Profitability

A utility company in Houston wants to sell electricity to a hand-full of customers at some 5% discount.[1] These customers in an experimental tariff would pay for energy on a 'real-time' basis, prices that reflect the costs of generating the power now (or in real time). Since the cost of the power generation varies — rising at peak times and falling in non-peak hours — the new structure would allegedly allow the customers more control over their costs. Thus, power companies could use price to shift customers away from peak times and delay building additional generating capacity.

---

1. Houston Business Journal, Vol. 25 No. 45: *HL&P Seeking Special Rates for 100 Business Customers*, Ann de Rouffignac.

You can find an example of the actual current cost of electricity on the HL&P website. That address is http://www.hlp.com. Potential customers can decide if they would benefit from signing up on this program with a customer-specific charge. Central Power and Light and West Texas Utilities already use real-time pricing.

California Public Utilities Commission (CPUC) proposed a final rule to create a state agency that will buy energy from the lowest bidder. The proposal bypasses the independent provider, opting for a totally free market approach.

Some companies have moved to automated meter reading although the initial costs are high. Now that they have dropped to less than a $100 a meter, meter readers may never need to jump your fence again (or if you read your own meter — you won't have to anymore). This new meter automation also allows for alarm monitoring, temperature monitoring (freeze protection, gas monitoring and other services.

Futures

The free market tool called futures reached deep into the electric power market and emerged with a way for producers and consumers on large scales to hedge their future prices and minimize risk. Presently, the electricity futures market just emerging represents very little participation by the big boys but they are all looking at it. Farmers already know about futures or should know about them. Now they can trade with their peers. Probably most home consumers will never trade these financial tools but now the opportunity exists for you to trade the same way the giants in the industry trade.

The futures on the NYMEX (New York Mercantile Exchange) show how electricity is the perfect commodity: all electrons are the same as far as we are concerned and price volatility is high. Transmission access rules and bottlenecks cause basis problems — differences between the cash price and the futures price.

The futures contract uses a size of 736 megawatt-hours, what a large department store would use in a month. The contracts reach out to 18 months for a delivery time over one month. Since the grid is broken into West, East and Texas divisions, the national electric grid will not yet allow for a lot of electricity to be transmitted across it. And not all utility companies can utilize these financial instruments because of their charter. But the utility company can tell what its own generating costs are and what the current market is.

If you are interested in this subject, see the article "Bringing Electricity to the Market" in *Futures* magazine. Great stuff there.[1]

Capacity

Several questions plague the industry. What are the long-term energy availabilities? Most companies can provide energy beyond blips in the oil and gas prices short-term. But long-term problems arise when we look into your usage over the next few years combined with commercial usage. If you are a rural customer, you may begin to use alternative methods of power production (read that as "your own"). That could cut into profits of the big providers.

One of the alternate sources is wind. The LCRA, an Austin, Texas utility company serving customers in 50 counties, just finished a wind farm or turbine site in west Texas. They can enlarge the project twenty-fold if needed. The wind-generated power never ends and does not pollute. The output represents some 1% of all the LCRA output as of this writing.

Next the issue of *wheeling* or *deregulation*. Deregulation could mean that customers could buy from the company offering the most competitive rate, much like people buy long distance service.

---

1. Futures, *Bringing Electricity to the Market*, September, 1995. Reprints from Cynthia McKean, PARS International Corp./Futures at (212) 674-7871.

Wheeling allows free access to transmission lines. Pipelines use this concept to move gas around, paying transmission or 'shipping' fees. Electricity could be routed much the same way.

New companies want the right to move around their own power for their own use. Now, most excess power produced by industrials or homeowners must be sold to the local utility company at a predetermined price. The concept of moving electricity like gas companies do with their product as a generic scares the companies with lots of low profit users, much like the post office versus an overnight carrier. The upstarts can skim off the profitable accounts by enticing the best customers with low prices while leaving the old and less profitable sorts to the utility company.

The Lower Colorado River Authority worked with Destec and Enron to forge a contract allowing it to buy power competitively rather than build its own plant. New Texas regulations allow wholesale power generators to sell electricity to utilities and industrial customers without being regulated as a public utility. This too represents new and creative developments.

Finally, new patterns of usage with concern for wastage and inefficiency may reduce the current demand and slow the growth of electrical consumption trends in the future (declining incomes).

The Utility Workers Union opposes wheeling and *retail competition* because they believe that restructuring the most reliable electric system in the world will jeopardize jobs. They further believe that utility regulation should be left to the states, not federally mandated. Shades of junior high history classes.

Public Education

Call or write your utility company about the list of publications they prepare. The state regulatory commission will also distribute literature on the consumer guide to utility regulation, your rights as a customer, billing information and rates, metering and submetering, public hearings and rate cases. Dry subjects but the price of democracy is a vigilant public. If you are electronically astute, log onto the utility company website nearest you and learn about the goings on. Look at the National Rural Electric Co-op Association site. That address is http://www.nreca.org. It is linked to many other sites of real interest and importance to you as a consumer.

Alternative Capacity

Some companies can now venture into alternative production methods. Enron, for example, stepped into solar power production with a $150 million plant capable of producing 100 megawatts of solar power at prices half the going rate. This plan would convert the nuclear testing site in southeast Nevada into a *solar park* per requirements of the Department of Energy which wanted to buy the power produced. Enron would also have a manufacturing facility nearby to make the solar panels.

Behind the 'Coal Curtain'

The US Agency for International Development and the National Rural Electric Co-op Association with a consortium of others work to improve efficiency of energy production and use in Poland, Hungary, Slovakia, Romania, Bulgaria and Latvia, as well as Lithuania and Albania.

It looks like the utility companies awakened to their responsibilities and their potential. As with many things in America, we often grouse about the situation but America is really very open in so many ways. You can influence the quality of life for yourself and others through our way of life. But you must be knowledgeable or ask the right questions and you must be concerned. Then you must become active. Government is the ultimate way to achieve that activism.

What the Government Is Doing

Lighting manufacturer ally

If you have responsibility at your home or work for the lighting, please access the website address http://www.epa.gov. This is the EPA site which may also be reached at (202) 775-6650 for printed material on this subject.

With the new government program, we can now think of lighting as an *investment*. The United States Environmental Protection Agency established a **Green Lights Program** which helps participants get *30% return* on their investment! The assertion: reduce your "...lighting electricity bill by *more than half* while maintaining or improving lighting quality." They term it "pollution prevention at a profit."

If Green Lights were fully implemented in the U.S., they assert, "...the country would save 65 million megawatt-hours of electricity per year, reducing the national electric bill by $16 billion per year." These savings could then be invested in new jobs and enhanced productivity. In addition, Green Lights would result in reductions of carbon dioxide, sulfur dioxide, nitrogen oxides equivalent to 12 percent of U.S. utility emissions, curbing acid rain and smog..."[1]

The program differentiates between partners, allies and endorsers. Partners include corporations of all kinds, non-profits, governments, healthcare facilities, universities and colleges, restaurant and hotel chains. Participants sign a memorandum of understanding with the EPA which means they agree to survey 100% of their facilities and within 5 years to upgrade 90% of the square footage that can be upgraded profitably without compromising quality.

The EPA then provides a hotline, a lighting upgrade manual, training workshops, software analysis tools, a financing directory, current performance and price information on energy-efficient lighting products, ally programs which bring together members of the lighting industry and electric utilities to encourage customers to use energy-efficient lighting technologies and manuals and publications covering lighting technology and upgrade processes.

Energy Act of 1992

On October 31, 1995, the government instituted new standards for light bulbs in home and office settings. The actual legislation is known as the *Energy Policy Act of 1992*. A copy of this is also in the appendix for those interested. This legislation mandates that information be made available to the consumer and that the information will be based on *lumens per watt* rather than on watts alone.

Unfortunately, all this means that the rules changed and it is now harder to understand what to buy. For example, a bulb using 15 watts of electricity may now put out as much light (lumens) as a 60 watt incandescent, and cost several times more! The more expensive bulb may last longer and use less electricity: even though it costs more, it may be by far the better buy.

---

1. U.S. EPA website
   http://www.epa.gov/docs/GCDOAR/greenlights.html.

Deregulation

The National Energy Policy Act of 1992 authorized third party suppliers and independent power producers and marketers to be on equal footing with utility companies (which have traditionally controlled access to transmission lines).

Could it make the electric power industry more competitive? Deregulation occurred in the trucking industry, the banking industry and many others. Now it is headed for electricity. The issue hangs on the identity of the seller: who will a company, a resident and a government buy electricity from? Right now, customers buy from utility companies and must typically buy from the one who runs the wire to the location. In gas sales, gas goes in at one end of the line and comes out at your location and you can buy from almost anyone. The same could be done for electricity.

However, the rural electric companies must run more miles of wire and cable to reach remote locations while urban or industrial utility companies run a very short leg to the consumer. Look at it like mail delivery. The government has to provide you with mail, whether you live in a big city or a small road far away from town. It costs more to serve the little guy and the profit is less. Take away the big profit centers to offset the remote location losses and only losses are left. Not very satisfying for the rural or residential user.

Wheeling

The reselling of electricity to outside consumers received the tag *wheeling*. Utility companies with high fixed costs will logically resist change without some sort of protection from the companies slicing off the most profitable segment of usage. Wheeling will be possible soon for large industrial and government users. Legislators and lobbyists, consumers and residential users will have to sort out all the new possibilities in the coming years. This subject will be commonplace conversation in years to come.

Solar Plans

The Department of Energy is considering some thirty proposals to turn its nuclear testing site in southeast Nevada into a solar testing park. Enron suggested that the DOE (Department of Energy) offer to buy the plant's generated electricity. This plant as proposed by Enron would cost upwards of $150 million and produce 100 megawatts of power. That would effectively double the current U.S. production of commercially available solar power. The other major solar player in this arena is Siemens AG. The DOE seeks new ways to diversify the U.S. need for power to lessen the reliance on foreign oil and dependence on other governments for our power. Another factor, the output of polluting emissions, affects the equations. The DOE wants to cut the cost of photovoltaic power to 6 cents per kilowatt hour. Currently, the government pays about 5.5 cents per kilowatt hour. Solar power typically runs around 13 to 15 cents. Enron would also build a plant next door to manufacture the solar panels.

Acid Rain Pollution Credits

A federal law currently allows a company to buy and sell the right to pollute. It is a free market system for controlling emissions. So far, the plan has achieved only marginal success.

The Clean Air Act of 1990 cut allowable emissions of sulfur dioxide by roughly half. Supposedly, the new system would bring free economy forces to bear on the expensive road to pollution control. Other chemicals follow similar schemes to license the amount of pollution. If you generate less waste or control it for less, you can create a pollution credit and then sell it to someone else.

Sulfur Bulbs

The DOE helped develop a new form of electrodeless light bulb called a sulfur lamp. The DOE let a contract to inventor company Fusion Lighting, Inc. The closed quartz sphere bombards the amount of sulfur in one match head in an inert argon gas at one-tenth atmospheric pressure with microwaves. The bright illumination resulting resembles sunlight.

The argon heats up and vaporizes the sulfur which forms two atom molecules. When the excitation dissipates, a sunlight-like light emerges in large amounts in a wide spectrum or wavelengths. The sulfur gets very hot. Early models of the bulb rotated 300 to 600 rpm in some way to cool the quartz and keep it from destruction.

We are told that one sulfur bulb using microwave-like radiation generates as much light as hundreds of conventional bulbs. We have not yet seen one and do not expect residential and small commercial applications anytime soon but surprises can happen.

Energy Efficiency and Renewable Energy Clearinghouse

Also know as EREC, this operation offers information and assistance to a broad audience of consumers, educators and students, builders, business, governments and their agencies, entrepreneurs and organizations. They provide publications, customized responses and referral to energy organizations.

Conclusion

Now that we have "looked" at many ways of reducing our electric consumption, let's consider somethings in *enlightened* retrospect. We noted in the beginning that readers of this book *can* all pay the electric bills (for the most part without undue hardship) so *why* would we be willing to go to the trouble of doing all, or even part, of the "stuff" suggested in this book?

Obviously for the dollars and cents. We would save some money; it is not an immense amount, but some! And we will improve the general quality of our lives, particularly if we implement daylight balanced lights into our home and work environments.

But is there some further motivation which would make going to all this trouble more worthwhile? Until recently (and I am no kid anymore) I would have thought no further. But since writing this book, I have learned a lot and I suggest that you and I should look further into our motivations. Two reasons emerged.

First, fossil fuels are a finite, limited resource. Even if we had two or three times what we know about now, the time of depletion would only be shoved back twenty or thirty years at the present rate of consumption! I find that thought sobering when I really think about it. Yes, we do have alternatives on the drawing boards — fusion energy, hydrogen from water and other ideas — but the actual depletion of oil and gas — wow!

The second reason arises independent of the availability of fossil fuel. It has to do with the deforestation worldwide of forests and rainforests and the amount of carbon dioxide each of us puts into the atmosphere as we use electricity, gasoline, natural gas and wood in our fireplaces. The forests and rainforests have been turning carbon dioxide into oxygen for eons. Much of this primeval forest will soon be cleared for people to live and raise cattle for the U.S. market. When the rainforests are cleared and (usually) burned, they stop producing oxygen; more carbon dioxide is produced. Carbon dioxide adds to the greenhouse effect, the trapping of the sun's energy in the atmosphere of the earth.

The consequences of this tremendously increased greenhouse effect in the last two decades or so probably results in global warming. Eighteen million years ago, the oceans were about four degrees Fahrenheit cooler than today. That warming has been quite slow, especially when compared to the warming that may take place in the next two decades. A four degree rise in ocean temperatures would drastically alter global weather patterns. Sea levels would rise significantly, as much as five feet, inundating most of the coastal cities. Hurricanes would become more severe and far more destructive.

I don't want to sound like a doomsayer but there are some substantial benefits to us and other human beings on the planet if we individually conserve electricity — something that can be done by anyone old enough to turn off a water faucet or light switch.

Appendix A:
Electricity and How It Works

You do not need to understand this appendix to lower your electric bill. However, if you do read and understand the information, you will definitely be a much better informed electricity consumer. I have worked very hard to keep this simple and understandable. I hope I have achieved that goal and that you will read and understand at least most of what I have presented here.

Please as least skim or look over this material. If you have trouble understanding it, try coming back sometime later. I have found that coming back later has been helpful to me in trying to understand things that were too difficult at first.

Fundamentals of Electricity

Electricity — how does it work, how can you save it? Good questions! Ones I shall try to answer in terms that most everyone can understand. When science was young, scientists thought that *static electricity* was a different and separate kind from the electricity that flowed in a wire. Scientists also believed that electricity was unrelated to magnetism.

Static electricity causes socks to stick together out of the dryer if no fabric softener has been added.

Moving electricity lights a bulb or turns a fan. Magnetism causes a compass to point north.

A brilliant Scotsman named Maxwell saw how they were all related to each other. He wrote down six equations which still explain the interrelationship of electricity (both static and flowing) and magnetism. These equations are the mathematical foundation of *all* of electricity, electronics and all the other technological wonders of today.

Since these equations are usually first discussed in college level engineering or physics, I won't attempt more than to give Maxwell the credit he is due here! However, I do want to explain some fundamentals so that everyone can understand a few basic principles.

Conductors and Insulators

Matter can be divided into three general categories:
* conductors,
* nonconductors or insulators and
* something in-between called semiconductors (what transistors and photovoltaic cells are made from).

Conductors, usually metals, have atoms with loosely attached electrons, usually one electron per atom. *Insulators* have atoms with *no* loosely attached electrons. It is the loosely-attached electrons that can move from atom to atom that become *electric current* when they move. This happens only in conductors.

Moving Electrons

What causes electrons to move? A great and fundamental question! The name of this force that causes electrons to move is *electromotive force* or *emf.* You can almost feel that the words in the name of this force almost say move electrons. And that is exactly what emf does! Moving electrons are what we call *electric current*.[1] The term we use to describe the emf is *voltage*.[2] *Current* is measured in amperes or amps, *voltage* is measured in *volts*. Remember: voltage causes electrons to move; current results when the electrons do move.

How many electrons move when a current flows? The number will give you a headache just trying to visualize it — "one" followed by about 24 zeros: 1,000,000,000,000,000,000,000,000 roughly, and this is just for a small current!

Resistance or Load

I mentioned above that the electrons were "loosely" attached in conductors. This doesn't mean that they are *not* attached. It takes some *pull* (or emf, alias voltage) to move them. It is the overcoming of this attaching force that results in what we call *resistance*. The greater the resistance, the greater the voltage required to move electrons. Insulators, whose electrons are very strongly attached, do not conduct current unless the voltage is *very, very high*. On the other hand good conductors like copper or silver will "conduct" current with a very *small* emf.

What does all this mean? That the wires in your house are conductors, usually copper. Also the inside of the cords you plug into the wall socket are good conductors. And the stuff on the outside, that keeps you from getting shocked when you touch the cord is insulation.

How Electricity is Created

So how does an emf come about? When an object is moved through a magnetic field (or a magnetic field is moved across an object) an emf is induced. If the object is a wire, a good conductor, the emf will result in a current, if the wire is a part of a closed circuit or loop.

When an object is moved through a magnetic field, an emf is induced.

1. Current is measure in Amperes or amps.
2. Voltage is measured in volts or thousands of volts i.e. kilovolts, or thousandth of a volt, i.e. millivolt.

In Figure A-1, A Simplified Generator, the magnet spins around inside the loop of wire. This moving magnetic field induces an emf in the loop of wire which causes a current to flow through the entire circuit. The resistor is the load.

Figure A-1, A Simplified Generator.

Figure A-2, Another simplified generator with slip rings.

Since there is a load, the spinning of the magnet will require an effort—it will not spin freely. It will require some kind of torque to keep it spinning. In your car, it is the gasoline engine that turns the "generator" (and moves the car too). In a power plant, it might be a steam turbine. At a hydroelectric plant it would be the force of the water behind the dam.

Figure A-1 shows a magnet spinning inside a loop of wire. Figure A-2, another simplified generator, shows a loop of wire spinning between the poles of a stationary magnet! The zigzag mark is a symbol for the resistor. Both of these types of arrangements will generate electricity and are actually used in electrical devices. Of course, there are many variations and refinements of these basic approaches in the actual devices in use today.

How Electricity is Used

...the only difference (in principle) between a motor and a generator is whether it is driven or it drives!

Now that we have found out how to generate electricity, we shall look into how it can be used! Now listen carefully! If we take the output of one of the generators in Fig A-1 or Fig A-2 and connect it to a device made exactly like it, the second identical device will become an electric motor! Let me say that again: the only difference (in principle) between a motor and a generator is whether it is driven or it drives!

Direct Current and Alternating Current

The electric utility industry was founded in 1882. It was then that American genius Thomas Edison figured out the things I have just explained. He invented the first commercial generator. He generated direct current (DC) electricity that only goes in one direction. I suppose he used DC because is easier to understand than alternating current (AC). AC goes back and forth, changing the direction of current flow sixty (60) times per second! Anyway, Edison had not figured out everything about electricity at that time. As a result he could only send his electricity about a mile before it became almost useless (from transmission losses). More on this later.

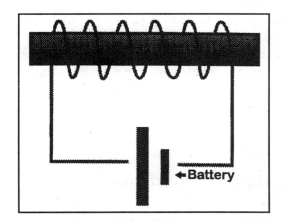

Figure A-3, Electromagnets.

Magnets and Electromagnets

There are naturally occurring magnets such as *lodestone,* an iron-rich mineral. Man has discovered how to make magnets, too. One kind retains its magnetism and is called a permanent magnet. The other is non-permanently magnetized. This type is only a magnet when current is flowing around it — an *electromagnet.* When no electric current flows through its wire coils, it is only slightly magnetic. Figure A-3: *Electromagnets* shows electromagnets. The earth itself is a magnet. The north pole is up north and the south pole is down south (surprisingly enough). The north magnetic pole is not at the geographical north pole or spin axis of the earth, however. The north magnetic pole is somewhere in far, north-central Canada.

Magnetic Fields and Their Effects

The most important property of any magnet is its magnetic field. This field can be thought of as

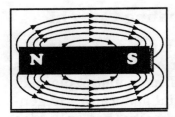

Figure A-4 shows the pattern of lines of force.

being composed of lines of force leaving the north pole of the magnet and propagating all through space in all directions with each one ending up at the south pole of the magnet. See Figure A-4 which shows the pattern of the lines of force.

The number of lines of force can be considered as a measure magnetic strength. A strong magnet would have lots of lines-of-force while a weak magnet would have only a few. Remember from our discussion of a generator above that lines of force (or the magnetic field) moving in relation to a conductor (wire) will generate an emf in that conductor. "In relation to" means either that the field is still and the wire is moving or that the wire is still and the field is moving (or both could be moving). If the magnetic field is from an electromagnet, then when the current is shut off, the magnetic field collapses. Now a collapsing magnetic field means the lines of force are moving. This, too, will cause an emf in a wire. (See the discussion of the distributor in your car below.)

As you can see there are many, many variations of all these combinations of fields, conductors, emfs and currents. Let's discuss some examples that you are probably familiar with.

Traffic Signal "Trigger"

When you come up to a left turn signal, have you noticed that there is a rectangle about the size of a car near the "stopping place? It is usually painted over with tar or epoxy or something. The traffic people have cut slots in the concrete and laid a big coil of wire down in the slot (then covered it with tar or something else to protect it from the traffic). We know that the earth is a big magnet, so there is a magnetic field going through that coil of wire in the concrete.

One of the properties of magnetic material, like iron (or steel, since it is mostly iron), is that it collects magnetic lines of force. It concentrates the lines of force in the immediate area around itself. In other words, the lines of force from the earth's magnetic field are changed from their more or less uniform spacing and are concentrated or collected by iron or steel. The larger the piece of iron, the more "lines" it collects.

As a result of this phenomenon, a car moving through the earth's magnetic field results in a concentration of lines of force going through the car and moving with the car. Thus, when a car drives up to a signal that has a (trigger or) coil in the concrete, the result is a disturbance of the *local magnetic field*. As the car approaches, the field inside the coil becomes weaker. This is because the lines-of-force are moving out toward the car (which "collects them").

When the car gets over the coil, the field is much stronger, with many more lines of force. This is due to the iron in the car that has "collected" them from all around. This change in the magnetic field causes a current in the coil at the signal. The current tells the signal controller that a car is there.

This might seem complicated but it really is simple when you think about it for awhile.

Telephone

Another example is the telephone. When you talk, your vocal cords make sound waves which go through the air and into the telephone mouthpiece. Inside, the sound waves cause a magnet to move back and forth through a coil of wire. The current generated from this movement is sent over the wires to a receiver at the other end of the telephone line. The current runs through another coil. The current in the coil at the receiving end causes a magnet to move a "speaker" diaphragm. The "speaker" diaphragm generates sound waves just "like" your voice did at the transmitting end of the line.

The Ignition System in Your Car

In your car, the ignition system "fires" your spark plugs causing the gasoline and air to burn and turn your engine. A spark plug usually requires about 35,000 volts to fire properly. If you are even a little bit familiar with the workings of your car, you know that the battery and most of the rest of the electrical system is 12 volts! So how does 12 volts get changed to 35,000 volts to fire the spark plugs?

When you start your car, the engine starts to turn. The engine is connected to a distributor which directs the high voltage to the right spark plug at the right time. A "switch" opens and closes as the engine rotates. When the switch is closed, the battery is connected to the "low voltage" side of the ignition coil.

The low voltage side of the coil has a "few" turns of copper wire around an iron core. There also, around the same core are "many" turns of fine wire. The "many turns" end is connected from the coil to the distributor. Now when the switch in the distributor opens the current in the low voltage part of the coil stops! (Amazing isn't it!) But when the current stops in the coil, the magnetic field that it had been inducing collapses. When the field collapses from the low voltage coils, it has to collapse through the many turns of the high voltage coil! This magnetic field from the few turns and high current of the low voltage parts induces about the same voltage in each turn of the (many) turns of the high voltage coil. Since the coil is one piece of wire wound "round 'n round," the voltage in each turn is added to the next turn of the coil. By the time all the voltages from each turn are added together, it adds up to about 35,000 volts!

Summary

The examples could go on and on. There are, of course, many refinements and much sophistication in the devices of today, Ultimately, however, their roots go back to Maxwell's equations and the interactions of magnetic and electrical fields. It all is a result of electric currents and magnetic fields. There are electric fields, too, which are explained by Maxwell's equations. However, when you start to consider all the detailed interactions, it gets really complicated fast. The basic principles are similar to what we have discussed here.

*Figure B-1, Typical
Transformers.*

Appendix B:
How does the electricity
in your house work?

Transformers

Edison's first generator was DC. He could not transmit electricity over a mile because of transmission losses. AC (or alternating current) voltage can be "transformed" higher or lower through a device called (surprisingly enough) a transformer (see Figure B-1 Typical Transformers).

Since it is AC, the current is going back and forth 60 times every second. This causes expanding and collapsing magnetic fields, just like in the coil of your car. These changing fields cause a magnetic field inside the iron core of the transformer (because it is the path of least resistance for the magnetic field). When the magnetic field from the first coil passes through the second coil (which is also wrapped around the same magnetic core), it generates or induces a different current and voltage in this second set of transformer coils. The induced voltage is equal to the number of turns in the second coil divided by the number of turns in the first coil! Since the power has not changed, only the voltage, the current is changed inversely. If the voltage goes up, the current goes down! It is important to understand this. If it is not clear, try reading it again.

Transmission Losses

A basic principle of electricity shows that transmission losses are related to the current in the transmission line. In fact, they are proportional to the square of the current. This means that if you reduce the current to half, the losses are reduced[1] to one quarter. This is the reason that transmission lines on the electric towers in the country (and even around town) have very high voltages, like 460,000 volts!

House Power

Figure B-2,
Pole Transformer.

If you have an electric pole in your neighborhood, you will notice the round cylinder-shaped gadgets at the top of the pole (See Figure B-2: Pole Transformers). They might be a foot or two in diameter and two or three feet long and very likely will have finned surface to help with cooling. They will have a set of wires connecting the transformer(s) to the wires on the top of the pole (that go from pole to pole to pole). Another set of wires come out of the transformer to your house, your neighbor's house and so on.

If you live in a neighborhood with underground electricity instead of power poles, you will find big, usually green cubes along the route that the poles would take if they were there, probably along your back property line or alley if you have one. These cubes usually have fins on the vertical walls and are from 2 or 3 feet on a side to even larger dimensions. If you have underground wiring, you won't see the power coming into you house till you find the circuit breaker box, where it will enter up from under ground, usually inside of a wall. So just imagine what I describe in the next paragraph or go look at a neighborhood with power poles.

These wires, three of them, coming to your house are at *house power* or 240 volts, single phase. The wires at the top of the poles are at high transmis-

---

1. One half squared (i.e. times one half) is one quarter or one half of one half.

sion voltage, normally, over 10,000 volts. After going through a transformer, the voltage is tepped down to house voltage. When the wires get to your house, they will go through the utility company's meter and then into you circuit breaker panel, usually inside the house, but not always.

In the circuit breaker box, the 240 volt power is divided into two 120 volt lines. This is done by having one of the *hot* lines connected to one side of your breaker box and the other hot line connected to the other side. The third line from the pole is *neutral* and is connected to the middle of your breaker box. It is also connected to a piece of metal driven several feet into the ground and it is also called *ground*. It is at the same emf, voltage or potential as the earth itself. It is also at the same potential as neutral, too.

High Powered Home Electric Appliances

Your electric stove, electric dryer and electric hot water heater (if you have any of these) connect across both hot wires and thus are supplied with 240 volts. Almost everything else in your house is connected from one hot wire to ground, thus receiving only 120 volts.

The Rest of the House Circuits

If you have a reasonably new house, you will have outlets with two vertical slots and a third round hole either above or below the pair of slots. One of the slots is taller, wider or longer than the other. The bigger or wider slot connects to ground or neutral. The round hole is connected to ground. New electric appliances will have plugs with one prong wider than the other so that they can only be plugged into an outlet one way. This improves electrical safety by making sure that the parts of the appliance that you touch are connected to "ground" or "neutral" rather than to the "hot" wire. If you force the plug in backwards you could receive an electric shock from whatever you plugged in.

Safety

This brings us to another benefit of AC over DC.

Since the current reverses 60 times a second, the current in your body from a shock is not constant but back and forth with periods of no or zero current (when it changes from one direction to the other). This permits the muscles to release, let go or even jump. This means that if you get a shock from an AC circuit you can usually let go! With DC, the current never reverses. This sometimes causes the muscles to stay in spasm and never let go. This makes DC at high voltages (over about 50 volts) much more dangerous than AC. Of course, at really high voltages, both types can be fatal.

My adult daughter discovered this experimentally and accidentally. I was installing paneling and had an outlet pulled out from the wall. I would normally opened the circuit breaker that controlled this outlet but the computers and several other devices in use in the office were being used so I left it "hot" and exposed. My daughter has a toddler. Noticing that the outlet was not "plugged" by the plastic protectors, she grabbed the outlet to "plug it up" so the baby could not get into it. In so doing, she touched the black wire, which is "hot." She got a shock! It "hurt" or was at least very uncomfortable but did no harm whatsoever! Had it been DC at the same voltage it could have killed her because she might not have been able to let go. She learned to watch out for the black wires!

If you are around high voltage DC (over about 50 volts), never be alone! If you get caught by a DC wire, another person can separate you from the wire and perhaps save your life.

Two more safety tips. If you are working with electricity at home, wear rubber-soled shoes and keep one hand in your pocket. With one hand in your pocket, you won't be likely to make a complete circuit from one hand to the other. It takes only about 50 thousandth of an amp (milliamp, or *ma*) through the chest cavity to stop your heart! With rubber shoes and one hand, it is very unlikely that 50 milliamps can go through your chest.

Equipment Voltage Ratings

A few words here about the voltage ratings on the name plates of equipment and devices. The "120" volt rating is also equivalent to 107v, 110v, 115v, 117v, or nearly any other number near these values that someone may find on a name plate. Likewise, 240 may appear as 208v, 210v, 220v or 230v, while 480 may be shown as 440v or 460v. These are all equivalent to one of the three — 120, 240 or 480v. An exception is 277v — this the voltage between any two legs of a three phase 480 volt circuit. You may find other unusual voltages like something in the three hundred volt range. This would either be DC or equipment imported from Europe.

Other Electric Devices

Electrical devices include motors, lighting, heating, welders, x-ray machines and many, many others. I shall discuss a few of these that are widely used in the home or that have special implications. I have uncovered a few new or truly exceptional devices and pass on the phone numbers or addresses so that you may research these items for your possible use if you are interested.

Technology has brought us a vast array of electrical and electronic products that have the potential to reduce your bill. Please remember that I am only informing you of these devices, and giving you phone numbers or addresses. I am not recommending them. They may be ways for you to reduce bills, but you must be the ultimate judge of their efficacy and appropriateness for your home and situation.

Electric Motors

Their are electric motors in nearly every appliance (that isn't specifically used for heating) in your home. Electric motors have been designed for a myriad of uses, so naturally many designs and types are used in the home. Three main types make up the bulk of all electric motors.

By far the most common form of electric motor, the induction motor — the least expensive motor type — comes in a very wide variety of sizes and configurations. Although the speed does vary somewhat with load, induction motors are essentially constant speed devices. Characteristically, induction motors will also have high starting torque, as if you cared. They can be "totally enclosed," suitable for operation in explosive environments (another bit of "motor lore"). Incidentally, electrical devices for "turning or rotating" things are called *motors*. Internal combustion devices like the one in your car is called an engine, not a motor, technically.)

Induction motors usually have one of two common rotational speed ratings — 1725 and 3450. Most induction motors can have their direction of rotation reversed by physically changing wiring connections.

Continuously variable speed motors are direct current (DC) machines. Advantages: they can produce nearly any required torque at nearly any required speed. Their rotation can be reversed by reversing the polarity of the supply voltage. Remember that induction motors have to be rewired physically to reverse rotation. Thus they can go "backward" and "forward" by simply reversing the voltage. Disadvantage: electricity is supplied from the utility company in AC (alternating current) form and must be transformed into direct current. This transformation is called *rectification*.[1]

Synchronous motors, the third type, rotate at some multiple of one revolution for each cycle of the alternating current. They have a firmly fixed rotation speed. The electric clocks in you home, at least the old analog types, are powered by synchronous motors. They are as accurate as the utility company's speed control. Utility companies use an electronic cycle counter and compare it to a high-precision mechanical clock to ensure that their frequency is accurate and stable.

---

1. And again, once it is DC, its voltage cannot be changed.

Summary and Conclusion

In Appendix A and Appendix B, we have discussed some heavy concepts. We have talked about the units of electricity, talked about Maxwell's equations and gone into some of the properties of DC and AC circuits. This is an ambitious undertaking for a few pages. I hope that you have been able to absorb the main ideas presented, along with the relationships between the different parameters — don't you just love the wonderful engineering terms such as parameter? Honestly, it was several years after I first heard the term that I figured out that it just meant "variable" or a number that could be changed or something like that. It does have a wonderful sound though, doesn't it: PARAMETER! Wow! But on with the 'rat killing.' We should all know, or at least suspect, that

*   AC is used because its voltage can be changed upwards to reduce transmission losses and back down for home use. (The high voltage reduces the current and transmission losses, which are proportional to the square of the current.)
*   DC becomes quite dangerous at voltages over about 50V.
*   The voltages of the power lines around town are quite high, and consequently very dangerous.
*   That 120, 240 and 480 are the three common home or industrial voltage ratings.
*   That in a 120 volt circuit, only one wire is hot, the other(s) are at ground (zero voltage). Incidentally, codes require that the hot wire be black (or maybe red), the neutral (another word for ground) wire be white and the (sure-enough) ground wire be green (or bare). This might be useful if you ever take off a switch plate.
*   In a three-phase circuit there are usually four, but always at least three wires. With only three, all three are hot. With four wires, only the green is not hot.

So, as the sun pulls away from the shore and the ship sinks slowly in the west, we can now understand a lot of what has been discussed above.

Energy Audit

By auditing each room or component, you can consciously evaluate each application of power in your home to see if an improvement can be made. The object is to improve the quality of life while at the same time maintaining or reducing the consumption of electricity. By looking at each component, you will find out what your requirements really are and what might be done about them.

Air Conditioning

Actual Thermostat Setting:	
Summer (°F)	Winter (°F)

Recommended Thermostat Settings: Summer 78-80°F Winter 65-68°F

Locations of thermostats:	
Unoccupied facility	Temperature setting
Air filters changed	Next change
Seams and joints in air duct system checked for leaks?	
HVAC system balanced?	Which areas too hot?
Which areas too cold?	Number of A/C units?
Make:	Model:
EER:	Date of last service:

Heat Pumps

Number of heat pump units:	
Make:	Model:
EER:	Date of last service:

Central Heating/Central Heating Unit

Location:	
Make:	Model:
Date of last service:	Fuel used:
Age of boiler or furnace:	Age of burner:
Additional room heating appliances?	Ceiling fans installed?

Lighting

Be sure to examine lighting quality, safety and comfort levels in all areas including garage, utility rooms, closets, pet areas, livestock areas and shops.

Light fixture No. 1: (location)	
Bulb type, output:	Watts per square foot:
Light levels (too dim) (too bright)	How often are lights on?
Light switch accessible:	Timer appropriate:
Light fixture No. 2: (location)	
Bulb type, output:	Watts per square foot:
Light levels (too dim) (too bright)	How often are lights on?
Light switch accessible:	Timer appropriate:
Light fixture No. 3: (location)	
Bulb type, output:	Watts per square foot:
Light levels (too dim) (too bright)	How often are lights on?
Light switch accessible:	Timer appropriate:

Light fixture No. 4: (location)	
Bulb type, output:	Watts per square foot:
Light levels (too dim) (too bright)	How often are lights on?
Light switch accessible:	Timer appropriate:

Light fixture No. 5: (location)	
Bulb type, output:	Watts per square foot:
Light levels (too dim) (too bright)	How often are lights on?
Light switch accessible:	Timer appropriate:

Light fixture No. 6: (location)	
Bulb type, output:	Watts per square foot:
Light levels (too dim) (too bright)	How often are lights on?
Light switch accessible:	Timer appropriate:

Light fixture No. 7: (location)	
Bulb type, output:	Watts per square foot:
Light levels (too dim) (too bright)	How often are lights on?
Light switch accessible:	Timer appropriate:

Light fixture No. 8: (location)	
Bulb type, output:	Watts per square foot:
Light levels (too dim) (too bright)	How often are lights on?
Light switch accessible:	Timer appropriate:

Light fixture No. 9: (location)	
Bulb type, output:	Watts per square foot:
Light levels (too dim) (too bright)	How often are lights on?
Light switch accessible:	Timer appropriate:

Light fixture No. 10: (location)	
Bulb type, output:	Watts per square foot:
Light levels (too dim) (too bright)	How often are lights on?
Light switch accessible:	Timer appropriate:

Hot Water Heater

Electric?	Gas?
Temperature set at (°F)*	

*Recommended temperature 120°F, not higher than 140°F

Would alternative water heating be practical?	
Insulated jacket and pipes?	Heating volume adequate?

Windows

Weather-stripping:	Caulking:
Insulated glass:	Draperies:
Temperature barrier:	Reflective screen:
Solar film:	

Insulation

Ceiling:	Walls:
Floors:	Drafts present?
Foam wall outlet insulators installed?	
Cracks/Seams of different materials caulked?	

Appliances

List wattages, horsepower or efficiency ratings for each.

Refrigerator type, compressor rating, efficiency rating:	
Freezer type, compressor rating, efficiency rating:	
Oven:	Convection oven:
Stove:	Toaster:
Toaster oven:	Microwave:
Dishwasher:	Coffee pot:
Washer:	Dryer:
Sump pump:	Pond pump:
Pool pump:	Water pump:
Well pump:	Electric motors:

Air compressor:	Shop tools:
Computer:	Printer:
Copier:	Fax machine:

Notes:

Appendix C:
Electronic Forums

CD-ROM

Home Power Magazine
P. O. Box 520
Ashland, OR 97520
(916) 475-0830

Electric Power Energy

http://www.newspage.com/NEWSPAGE/cgi-bin/
walk.cgi/NEWSPAGE/info/d13/d4/

Energy Design Online

Energy efficient building BBS (212) 662-0338

Energy Efficiency and Renewable Energy Network (Department of Energy)

http://www.eren.doc.gov/season2.html

EPA Green Lights Program

US EPA
401 M Street, SW
Washington, DC 20460
(202) 775-6650
http://www.epa.gov/GCDOAR/GreenLights.html

Hourly electricity pricing

Houston Lighting & Power
http://www/hlp.com

NRECA

http://www.nreca.org
links to other related sites

Redwood Alliance

Redwood Alliance, P O Box 293, Arcata, CA 95518. (707) 822-7884.
E-mail: redwood.alliance@homepower.org

Energy issues locally, regionally, nationally; will put your organization on-line

Sources

Air Conditioning

ThermoRider, Inc. 6060 Richmond #305, Houston, Texas 77057 (713) 787-9910

Directory of Certified Unitary Air Conditioners and Unitary Air-Source Heat Pumps. Air Conditioning and Refrigeration Institute, 501 Wilson Blvd., Siute 600, Arlington, VA 22209

Directory of Certified Room Air Conditioners Association of Home Appliance Manufacturers, 20 N. Wacker Dr., Chicago, IL 60606

Associations

National Rural Electric Cooperative Association,
4301 Wilson Road, Arlington, VA 22203.
(703) 907-5664.

Cogeneration

Intelligen™ Energy Systems, Inc., 98 South St.,
Hopkinton, MA 01748. (508) 435-9007.

Geothermal

Geothermal Heat Pump Consortium,
c/o NRECA (703) 907-5664.

Green Lights Program

Green Lights Program, US EPA,
401 M Street, SW, Washington, D.C. 20460.
(202) 775-6650.

Heating

Steibel Eltron (Electric Thermal Storage
Heating) P. O. Box 40, Tioga Center, NY 13845.
(800) 582-8421.

Home Energy

Home Energy Magazine, 2124 Kittredge St #95,
Berkley, CA 94704. (510) 524-5405.

Home Power Magazine, P.O. Box 520, Ashland,
OR 97520. (916) 475-0830.

Lighting and Sensors

DuroTest Lighting, 9 Law Dr., Fairfield NJ
07004, (800) 289-3876

Genlyte Controls, Garland, Texas.
(214) 840-1640.

Home Automation Systems, Inc., 151 Kalmus Dr., L-4, Costa Mesa, CA 92626. (714) 708-0610.

Lighting Research Center NLPIP publications (specifier reports: exit signs, occupancy sensors, reflector lamps and other. (518) 276-8716.

MYTECH, 706 Brentwood St, Austin, Texas 78752-4042. (512) 450-1100.

National Lighting Product Information Program, Specifier Reports Abstract, Rensselaer Polytechnic Institute.

Solar

Aurora Power & Design, 3412 N. 36th St., Boise, ID 83703. (208) 368-0947.

BP Solar, Inc., P O Box 4587, Houston, TX 77210-4587. (713) 560-8681.

Backwoods Solar Electric Systems, 8530-HP Rapid Lightning Creek Road, Sandpoint, Idaho 83864. (208) 263-4290.

Offline Independent Energy Systems, P. O. Box 231, North Fork, CA 93643. (209) 877-7080.

Real Goods Trading Corporation, 966 Mazzoni Street, Ukiah, California 95482. (800) 762-7325. *Author's note: Exceptionally good source for all environmentally sound devices and technology.*

S&H Alternative Energy Products, RD3 Box 312, Putney, VT 05346. (802) 722-3704.

Seventh Generation® 1 Mill St. Box A-26, Burlington, VT 05446-1672. (800) 456-1177.

Solar Industry Journal, 122 C Street, NW, 4th Floor, Washington, DC 20001. (202) 383-2600

Solar Village Institute, 5840 Jewell Rd., Graham, NC. (800) 376-9530. Solar, wind and hydropower systems.

Solarex, Southwest Photovoltaic (PV) Systems, Inc., 212 E. Main St, Tomball, TX 77375. (713) 351-0031.

Staber Industries, 4411 Marketing Place, Groveport, OH 43125. (614) 836-5995.

Water

Pure Water, Inc., 3725 Touzalin Ave., PO Box 83226, Lincoln, Nebraska 68501. (800) 875-5915.

Wind

Southwest Windpower, 2131 1st St., Flagstaff, AZ. (520) 779-WIND.

World Power Technologies, Inc. 19 North Lake Avenue, Duluth, MN 55802. (218) 722-1492.

Glossary of Power Terms

Amps or **Amperes** - Electrical flow (similar to water flow in cubic feet per second) but in electrical terms

Btu - standard unit in measuring heat content of fuel. Btu stands for British thermal unit, the amount of heat needed to raise the temperature of 1 pound of water 1 degree Fahrenheit.

Color Temperature - Measured to determine light quality. Measured in degrees Kelvin (°K) with a theoretical black body or perfect radiator as the benchmark.

CRI - Color Rendering Index (see International Color Rendering Index).

Degrees Kelvin - the temperature a blackbody or perfect radiator would have to be heated to generate that particular color of light.

Demand charges - Demand meters measure the peak rate at which energy was consumed, as opposed to the quantity of energy consumed. Based on the highest average rate of electricity used by the customer over any 15-minute period during the billing period.

Foot candle - Measurement of illumination equal to one lumen per square foot, also the amount of light spread over a square-foot surface by one candle when all parts of the surface are one foot from the candle light source. Foot candle levels indicate only amount of illumination or intensity which is not the same as visual performance. With full spectrum light, the foot candle reading may be very low and yet give the same visual performance as high cool-white fluorescent light readings.

Frequency - The period of a current alternating. In the United States we use 60 cycles per second or 60 Hz.

International Color Rendering Index - (CRI) the way colors appear under a lamp compared to a reference source. Also know as "seeability" scale, running from 1 to 100. All colors appear true under daylight (100) which is based as the perfect light.

Kilowatt - one thousand watts. A watt is a unit of power.

Kilowatt-hour - Consumption of electricity is measured in kilowatt-hours (kw) which is the amount of energy delivered by an hour-long flow of 1 kilowatt of electric power. Your electric bill is based on the number of kilowatt-hours you use. A 100-watt bulb burning for 10 hours will use one kilowatt hour of electric power (100 watts multiplied by 10 hours equals 1,000 watt-hours or 1 kilowatt-hour.

Narrow band - Ideal fluorescent or incandescent would provide for 5,000°K light and would require 24% less energy to produce than a cool white lamp and 44% less energy than the warm white fluorescent.

Ohm - An electrical unit of resistance. Think of it as the diameter of a hose or pipeline.

Scotopic sensitivity - The ability to sense in darkness. In humans, scotopic sensitivity derives from the rod receptors in the eye, as opposed to the cone receptors which sense color at higher light levels. Scotopically rich light can allow things to be seen in the dimmest of conditions and need less photopic or daylight luminance to achieve a given level of visual acuity. Good colored light allows things to be seen in very low light levels. Thus lighting designed only on brightness will be less than optically satisfactory.

Spectral Power Distribution - Quantity of light or power emitted at each wavelength. Used to determine color temperature, color rendering index and lumen output of a particular lamp. The SPD of each major lamp type is measured by spectroradiometers.

Spectroradiometer - Device that breaks up light into individual components and measures the energies of the light spectrum.

Spinning Reserves - If demand outstrips supply, a generating facility needs spinning reserves. These are generators already spinning to produce power quickly.

Thermal Efficiency - Light produces heat. Some light sources produce less heat than others for the same amount of light. Incandescent sources typically generate 94% of the energy received as heat while compact fluorescent generate far less heat for the same amount of light.

Visual Clarity - Combines two features of scotopically richer light: the increased brightness perception for the same luminance and greater depth of field resulting from vision through smaller pupils. Both scotopic and photopic spectra affect visual acuity and that scotopically rich illumination is preferred. Application: A common fluorescent lamp fixture using four 34W cool white lamps could be replaced with two 47W lamps of scotopically rich narrow band bulbs in a more thermally-efficient way and produce more suitable light for humans and animals.

Volts - Electrical pressure (much like water pressure in pounds per square inch). One volt applied to a circuit with one ohm of resistance will produce one amp of current.

Watt - Electrical power (similar to horsepower measured in force per minute)

Wheeling - access to lines of distribution for transmitting power from area to area. Usually used in reference to competitive availability of electricity.

Bibliography

Backwoods Home Magazine, 1257 Siskiyou Blvd. #213, Ashland, OR 97520.

Berman, S.M., Jewet, D.J., Fein, G., Saika, G., and Ashford, F., *Photopic luminance does not always predict perceived room brightness*. Lighting Research Technology, Vol. 22, No. 1, pp. 37-41, 1990.

Directory of Certified Unitary Air Conditioners and Unitary Air-Source Heat Pumps. Air Conditioning and Refrigeration Institute.

Futures, Bringing Electricity to the Market, September, 1995. Reprints from Cynthia McKean, PARS International Corp./Futures at (212) 674-7871. Oster Communications, 219 Parkaade, PO Box 6, Cedar Falls, Iowa 50613.

Green Living Staff. (1994). Energy Efficient and Environmental Landscaping. South Newfane, VT: Appropriate Solutions Press.

Home Power Magazine. (1995). Ashland, OR: Home Power.

Potts, Michael. (1993). The Independent Home (Living With Power From the Sun, Wind and Water). Ukiah, CA: Chelsea Green/Real Goods Independent Living Books.

Rural Electrification Magazine. NRECA: Arlington, VA.

Self Reliant Intentional Communities Journal of Cooperative Living. Rt. 4 Box 169, Louisa, VA 23093. (703) 0894-5126. Quarterly. $18/yr.

Solar Electric Independent Home. Fowler Solar Electric, 226 Huntington Road, P.O. Box 435, Worthington, MA 01098. (413) 238-5974.

Solar Electricity Today. PV Network News, 2303 Pedros Circle, Santa Fe, NM 87505. Current dealers, manufacturers and information sources. $10.

Solar I. Home Power: Ashland, OR. 1995. Solar, Hydro, Wind, EV's, Home Power and Renewable Energy Sustainability Shareware CD-ROM. (1994). Home Power, P.O. Box 520, Ashland, Oregon 97520. (916) 475-0830. On magazines, back issues, shareware articles and providers, miscellaneous information.

Solar Industry Journal. 122 C Street, NW, Fourth Floor, Washington, DC 20001. Quarterly publication of the Solar Industries Association. $25.

Tynan, Tom. (1995). Step-By-Step, 15 Energy Saving Projects. Alvin, Texas: Swan Publishing.

UtilityFree™ Source Book. 74 Sunset Dr, #D, Basalt, CO 81621. (303) 927-1331. utilfree@infosphere.com

Index

cut here ✂

Understanding & Reducing Your Home Electric Bill

Richard Hepburn, B.S., M. S.
Edited by Christopher Carson & Patrick Zale

I want to comment on the book, tell you about new products or ideas. See my notes below.

_____
_____
_____
_____
_____
_____
_____
_____

Name: _____ Firm: _____

Address (no P.O. box): _____

City: _____ State: _____ Zip: _____

Telephone: _____

Emerald Ink Publishing • 7141 Office City Drive Suite 220 • Houston, TX 77087

Understanding & Reducing Your Home Electric Bill

Richard Hepburn, B.S., M. S.
Edited by Christopher Carson & Patrick Zale

Please send me _____ additional copies of **Understanding & Reducing Your Home Electric Bill** at $19.95 per book. Add $4.00 a book for priority shipping. Texas residents add 8.25% sales tax. Immediate shipment guaranteed.

Name: _____ Firm: _____

Address (no P.O. box): _____

City: _____ State: _____ Zip: _____

Telephone: _____

Payment:

_____ Check or money order enclosed.

Visa or MC Account#: _____

Exp. Date _____ Signature: _____

Emerald Ink Publishing • 7141 Office City Drive Suite 220 • Houston, TX 77087

POOR RICHARD'S ENERGY UPDATE

Please send me a *free* sample issue of **Poor Richard's Energy Update**. I understand that this is a free copy and I am under no obligation for any thing more than this free copy.

Name: _____ Firm: _____

Address (no P.O. box): _____

City: _____ State: _____ Zip: _____

Telephone: _____

Emerald Ink Publishing • 7141 Office City Drive Suite 220 • Houston, TX 77087

Poor Richard's Energy Update

Ben Franklin's *Poor Richard's Almanack* is long since gone but its spirit lives on with *Poor Richard Hepburn's Energy Update*. Everyone told him to go fly a kite so he did, figuratively speaking.

For a free issue of Poor Richard's Energy Update, call (800) 324-5661

or write

Emerald Ink Publishing
7141 Office City Drive, Suite 220
Houston, Texas 77087-3722

There is no obligation. We welcome your comments and suggestions, too.